Buy, Rent, and Sell

D1279960

Other McGraw-Hill Books by Robert Irwin

Home Buyer's Checklist

Home Closing Checklist

Home Renovation Checklist

Home Seller's Checklist

How to Buy a Home When You Can't Afford It

How to Find Hidden Real Estate Bargains

How to Get Started in Real Estate Investing

How to Invest in Real Estate with Little or No Money Down

Rent to Own

Tips and Traps for Getting Started as a Real Estate Agent

Tips and Traps for Making Money in Real Estate

Tips and Traps for New Home Owners

Tips and Traps When Building Your Home

Tips and Traps When Buying a Condo, Co-Op, or Townhouse

Tips and Traps When Buying a Home

Tips and Traps When Mortgage Hunting

Tips and Traps When Negotiating Real Estate

Tips and Traps When Renovating Your Home

Tips and Traps When Selling a Home

Buy, Rent,
and
Sell

*How to Profit by Investing
in Residential Real Estate*

Second Edition

ROBERT IRWIN

New York   Chicago   San Francisco   Lisbon London   Madrid Mexico City
Milan   New Delhi   San Juan   Seoul   Singapore   Sydney   Toronto

The **McGraw·Hill** *Companies*

Copyright © 2008 by The McGraw-Hill Companies, Inc. All rights reserved. Printed in the United States of America. Except as permitted under the United States Copyright Act of 1976, no part of this publication may be reproduced or distributed in any form or by any means, or stored in a database or retrieval system, without the prior written permission of the publisher.

2 3 4 5 6 7 8   DIG/DIG   15 14 13 12

ISBN 13: 978-0-07-148237-0
ISBN 10: 0-07-148237-7

This publication is designed to provide accurate and authoritative information in regard to the subject matter covered. It is sold with the understanding that neither the author nor the publisher is engaged in rendering legal, accounting, futures/securities trading, or other professional service. If legal advice or other expert assistance is required, the services of a competent professional person should be sought.

—*From a Declaration of Principles jointly adopted by a Committee*
of the American Bar Association and a Committee of Publishers

McGraw-Hill books are available at special quantity discounts to use as premiums and sales promotions, or for use in corporate training programs. For more information, please write to the Director of Special Sales, Professional Publishing, McGraw-Hill, Two Penn Plaza, New York, NY 10121-2298. Or contact your local bookstore.

This book is printed on acid-free paper.

Contents

Preface

Welcome to the second edition of *Buy, Rent, and Sell*, your complete guide to investing in residential real estate.

The first edition came out just as the so-called real estate bubble of the early 2000s began, and it made quite a splash. For some it quickly became the investing bible that led them to making quick fortunes in the market.

But the market never continues forever in any one direction. Thus this second postbubble edition has been completely updated and rewritten to help investors take advantage of a slipping market as well as a second wave of buying.

This new edition of *Buy, Rent, and Sell* shows you how to take advantage of new market conditions—how to find and buy foreclosures, bid at auctions, flip properties, and make lowball offers that get accepted. In short, once again it gives you, the investor, everything you need to turn a healthy profit in real estate.

Making money on real estate investments may sound simple, but the devil is in the details. Finding an advantageous property to *buy* can take great skill and patience. You might have to bid on several to get a good one. (And you'll have to know *when* to quickly flip a property.) To successfully *rent* out the property requires endurance, common sense, and knowledge. And then to *sell* the property for a profit, especially when the market is slower, often entails cleverness and sometimes flair.

Of course, thousands do it every day, and they make enough money in the process to quit their day jobs and, in many cases, even retire. The potential for making profits in real estate investments is big. It's just a matter of finding out how to get to those potentially profitable properties.

That's what this book offers: clear-cut examples, guidelines, and tips and traps.

Read it cover to cover or move to the chapter that best fits your situation. Either way, I hope you'll find it informative, productive, and worth many times over the cover price.

Good fortune in your real estate investing!

Robert Irwin

Buy, Rent, and Sell

Getting Started

Today's Real Estate Opportunities

When someone tells you it's the right time to buy, either it is the right time to buy, or it's the seller's right time to sell!

I recently received a call from an investor friend asking me this question: "Where are the opportunities in real estate today?"

He had been investing in property for about four years, and he commented, "I can't find any more homes to flip, there aren't any apartment buildings around offering positive cash flow, condo conversion no longer works—where's the smart money in real estate going right now?"

I might have dismissed the question if he had been a beginner who wasn't willing to do his homework, but my friend had completed half a dozen deals in different types of property and had reaped significant rewards. He was not inexperienced but instead was a highly successful investor—he had made well over a million dollars in profit. If he couldn't find good deals, how could anyone else?

So we got together, and I looked at what he was looking at. And, indeed, from his perspective all the deals around did seem poor. But then again, he was using a dull pencil to make his calculations. Having done well in the past, he was now looking for no-brainers. He wanted deals in which, with a minimum of effort and risk, he could go in and quickly pull out at least two or three hundred thousand in profit.

Yes, he had done those in the past, but I pointed out that easy deals were anomalies—they do occasionally happen, but you can't really count on them. Most of his big deals had happened when the real estate market was soaring prior to 2006. Back then, you could expect almost any amount of money you could throw at real estate to come back in profits.

Today, the market wasn't nearly as hot. Not everything was going to be profitable as quickly. I explained that nevertheless, by careful investing, it was still possible to find good deals—in fact, excellent ones. Today, I told him, it was time for bread and butter deals, those that required a new attitude, some energy, and some effort.

Today's good deals weren't going to come over and kick him to get his attention. Instead, he had to go looking for them. I pointed out many areas where they could be found including these:

Opportunities Today in Residential Real Estate

- Foreclosures
- Fixer-uppers
- Apartments (for the longer term)
- Lowballing (in which you make very low offers that are accepted by the sellers)
- Auctions
- Single-family rentals (for the longer term)

He rolled up his shirt-sleeves, and together we went looking. Over the course of the next chapters, we'll discuss the kinds of good deals we found out there.

Before you jump into real estate investing, it's important to understand the background against which you, as a real estate investor, will be working in today's market. Too many people walk away from the field saying "It's over." "The good times have passed." "There aren't any good deals to be made."

While it's true that the hot market of a few years ago may have abated, at least temporarily, the basic conditions that caused it remain. Today enormous opportunities exist because of these background conditions, and understanding them will allow you to take advantage of the market.

Background Conditions That Benefit Real Estate Today

- A continuing housing shortage
- Inflation
- Lots of financing money
- A powerful economy

A Continuing Housing Shortage

The most pervasive influence on real estate is the housing shortage. This actually dates back to the days of the Great Depression.

Back in the 1930s, there were virtually no new homes built. The reason was obvious: Almost no one had the money to buy, so why build a home you couldn't sell?

The advent of World War II in 1940 brought this housing shortage to a head. The demand for military and family housing was enormous. The result was temporary housing in the form of Quonset huts and barracklike structures. Intended to last only a couple of years, they continued to be used in some areas into the 1980s and later.

After the war the country went into a housing boom cycle in answer to the shortage. Developers in almost every state built tens of thousands of small, economical homes. These sold for under $10,000 apiece, often using GI or Federal Housing Administration (FHA) (little or nothing down) financing. Today, there are entire suburbs of these small homes that often have just two or three bedrooms and one bath and around 1,200 to 1,400 square feet of living area.

You may come across these in your area and see them as an investment opportunity. Before buying, however, be aware that they were designed with a lifespan of around 40 years. Today, we're well over 20 years past that intended lifespan, so expect there to be major deferred maintenance and repairs coming due.

After the 1960s, the country pretty much caught up with the housing shortage, until the real estate recession of the 1990s. Then, because of a broad economic downturn, property once again simply stopped selling. Of course, there had been real estate recessions since the Great Depression, but none as severe as that which occurred in the 1990s. Prices in some areas of the country, such as Florida, New York, and California, dropped by as much as 30 percent. Again, few developers were inclined to build what they couldn't sell.

This building slowdown exacerbated the housing shortage, which then led directly to the tremendous housing boom after the turn of the century. After 2000, a shortage of homes coupled with strong demand from an expanding economy drove prices to the sky. In some areas price increases of 25 to 30 percent a year became common.

Builders jumped in again, although initially more slowly because they had been burned by the real estate recession of the 1990s. Homes were built, and we were on the way to answering the housing shortage. That trend lasted until about 2006 when prices got so high that the market collapsed. Buyers got scared off. Builders began facing foreclosures, and once again they began cutting prices and auctioning off homes. Of course, fewer new homes were built.

That brings us up to this writing. Today, we haven't come close to meeting the gap between demand and supply for housing in this country. There's still a huge shortage.

TIP

A housing shortage is the most positive background a real estate investor can have.

Think of the enormous influx of immigrants who have come to the United States over the past several decades and our own internal population growth just from our birth rate (the population of the United States is now over 300 million), and it's easy to see why the demand for housing is strong. Add to that all the decaying residential housing (single family and apartments) that's ending its useful life, and you quickly find that in most areas of the country, supplies are down.

Evidence of this trend can be seen in the large increase in rental rates in most areas over the last few years. (Of course, that means residential properties with positive cash flow will be appearing once again.)

The background market conditions created by the continuing housing shortage mean that there's likely going to be a strong demand for residential real estate for decades to come. In other words, any current slowdown is just a lull in the storm. In a few years expect to see prices and sales take off again.

How High Can They Go? Of course, some people think we've reached a ceiling. How could prices possibly go any higher?

When someone says that, I'm always reminded of a radio show I did back in the 1970s (a true story). Back in 1976 I was a guest on a talk radio show out of Los Angeles, the Hilly Rose show. I can still remember the host asking me with consternation, "How can the price of a house go higher?" At the time the average price for a house in the L.A. area was going for around $70,000, a seemingly incredible figure. It was obvious to him, as it was to most people, that prices simply couldn't go up. He said something like, "I live in one of the nicest areas, and my house is worth $125,000. I can't believe prices could ever go higher."

I smiled and said that believe it or don't, prices will indeed go higher.

I don't think he believed me. But he should have. Try to buy any house in L.A. for $125,000 today! (The median price is close to $500,000.)

I expect the same thing to happen again in the future.

Which brings us to another background feature that is always working on real estate: inflation.

Inflation

Inflation can be good for you as a real estate investor.

A number of years ago there was a popular trilogy of movies called *Back to the Future*. In Part III, the hero, Michael J. Fox, goes back to 1885, and there with the help of costar Christopher Lloyd, gets a time machine to work, thus bringing him back to the future.

It was a good movie. But as I was watching it, I kept asking myself, "How did he buy anything back then?"

It's one thing to take a time machine to the past. It's quite another to buy a hat or a pair of shoes or parts to fix a time machine in 1885. How did he buy anything?

This is not to say that things were expensive out West back then. A bath and a shave were probably 7 cents. A night at a hotel, 20 cents. A meal might cost a dime, and so forth. Things cost very little in terms of what we're used to today. But what did our hero pay for them with? I don't think merchants back then accepted Visa, American Express, or MasterCard.

Today's paper money wouldn't have done very well back in 1885 either. It wouldn't be recognized or accepted.

Did they take pocket change? Our "silver" coins are all virtually worthless, shiny base metal. Can you imagine a western saloon-keeper in 1885 accepting a Washington quarter (made of copper and nickel) in payment for a "slug of whiskey"? He'd bite the coin, determine it wasn't silver or gold, and throw the person who offered it out the door.

So how did our heroes buy anything?

Making Purchases in 1885

The answer is real money. For example, Michael J. Fox could have used pennies—not pennies from today but pennies from 1885.

In 1885 the accepted penny across the country was the Indian Head. (It was the precursor to our current Lincoln cent.) If our heroes had the foresight to get a roll of Indian Head pennies before they went ahead to the past, they probably could have done very well. One roll of pennies would undoubtedly have enabled them to buy everything they needed for several days. If they happened to pick up a "Double Eagle" ($20 gold piece) of the period, they'd have enough money to live royally for a week or more.

Think of it: A penny actually buying something substantial instead of just weighing down your pocket with unwanted change. Twenty dollars lasting weeks! Our heroes could have lived like royalty for next to nothing.

Well, not quite.

The truth of the matter is that they just couldn't go to a bank today and simply ask, "Indian Head cents, please." Or "I'll have a $20 gold piece." Even though those items are still authorized currency of the United States, they are available only from collectors and rare coin dealers. And a single Indian Head penny in even modestly good condition might cost 10 of today's dollars. A common date $20 gold piece could be close to 1,000 current dollars or more.

When comparing prices of yesterday with the present, this is the part of the story that is often overlooked. Not only did things cost far less in the past but the very money that was used to purchase them in the past costs far more today.

In short, many things from the past that survive to the present actually retain their original buying power. Rare coins are one good example. Real estate is another.

A Piece of History

When you buy a resale house or small apartment rental, you're buying a piece of the past. You're buying an item that was built 1, 3, 7, or 47 years ago.

When you compare today's price of that older structure with the price it cost brand new, you will find almost invariably that it costs more today in current dollars than it did back then. Just like a bath or a meal or a room from 1885, the house built 10 years ago costs far more to purchase today in current dollars then it did years earlier.

Like the Indian Head pennies or the Double Eagle $20 gold piece, that house retains its value, its buying power, through time.

Money's Loss of Value

Let's look at it from a different angle. Instead of considering that which retains buying power, such as a house, let's consider for a few moments that which loses buying power: money.

No reasonable person will argue with the assertion that the value of the current dollar has declined. There are many reasons for this decline, and they include the increasing size of our money supply, the borrowing that our nation does in the form of our national debt and foreign trade debt, and the real or controlled scarcity of certain commodities such as oil. However, no matter what the reason, the simple fact is that consistently since the founding of our country, our money has become worth less and less in terms of what it will buy. To say it another way, it takes more and more current money to buy the same item.

TIP

Don't completely trust what the government says in the consumer price index (CPI) and wholesale price index (WPI). Inflation is usually much higher. A few years ago when housing prices started moving upward very dramatically, the government statisticians changed the inflation indexes. Higher housing prices pushed the CPI rate into the double digits. In response to this increase, the government removed the price of buying a house from the CPI and instead substituted the cost of renting, a much lower and steadier figure, at the time. Thus the CPI could show a much lower level of inflation (although a false one if you happened to be buying a house).

The government even attempts to measure the overall decline of our currency. Each month the federal government releases the *consumer price index* (CPI) and the *wholesale price index* (WPI) that purport to measure the loss in buying power of the dollar when it is compared with the previous 1-month and 12-month periods.

CAUTION

Should there be a dramatic increase in the supply of housing, or should the number of people in this country who are looking to buy suddenly decline, it will adversely affect real estate.

The Unseen Effects of Inflation

All of which is to say that something that has been ongoing for a very long time (certainly since 1885 and a lot before then), inflation, isn't likely to change in the future. Inflation has been a steady companion since the birth of our country, and it's likely going to be with us for an equally long time in the future. Except for relatively short periods (such as during the Great Depression), it's a constant that we need to accept and deal with.

The problem is that it has become unfashionable to speak of inflation. Back in 1980 when the government's CPI showed inflation to be running at an annual rate of 12 percent, it was on everyone's lips. Recently, however, with it running around 2 or 3 percent, few people worry about it. Mention inflation and many people will yawn. They've already heard that story.

But although 3 percent inflation is a lot less than 12 percent, it is still an enormous rate and can have an immense impact on pricing, particularly in real estate.

The Rule of 72

To see how inflation works in housing prices, let's use the *rule of 72*. In case you're not familiar with it, the rule of 72 allows you to approximately determine how quickly your money will double at any given interest rate. To apply this rule, you divide the interest rate into 72, and that gives the number of years that it takes to double your money. For example, at 10 percent interest, your money doubles in about 7.2 years. At 4 percent interest, it takes roughly 18 years, and so forth.

We can also use the rule of 72 to factor inflation into our calculations. If the rate of inflation is 6 percent, then our money will lose half its value in about 12 years ($12 \times 6 = 72$). If the rate of inflation is 3 percent, it will take about 24 years to lose half its value ($24 \times 3 = 72$).

Since the end of World War II, the rate of inflation in the United States has averaged around 5 percent. That means that every 15 years or so, our money loses half its value. A 2007 dollar, in other words, is worth roughly about 10 cents in terms of the buying power of a 1946 dollar. To put it another way, you need around 10 of today's dollars to equal the buying power of 1 dollar back in 1946.

Now what does this say for real estate?

The long-term trend in inflation in this country means that when a house costs half a million dollars today, it isn't as much money as most of us suppose. For example, 500,000 of today's dollars is only about 50,000 in 1946 dollars. It's not just that houses have gone up in price because of shortages and increased demand (as we've seen); it's also because of the fact that our money is simply worth less and it takes more of it to buy the same commodity.

Buying Power

Consider again the film *Back to the Future*. When Michael J. Fox was in 1885, what could he have brought back to the present that would have made him rich beyond his wildest dreams?

Obviously he could have brought back some Indian Head pennies and sold them for 10 current dollars apiece. Or he could have brought back $20 gold pieces and sold them for 1,000 current dollars apiece.

But what he could have brought back that would have made him even more fabulously wealthy is a deed. He could have brought back a deed to property in downtown Denver or San Francisco. He could have brought back a deed to virtually any piece of property anywhere, which he could have bought then for perhaps $100 or less and then sold it today for hundreds of thousands if not millions of dollars. Can you imagine what any piece of property bought in 1885 would be worth today . . . anywhere at all in the country?!

It's really from the perspective of the past that the true value of real estate, in this case investment, becomes clear. If property bought in 1885 would be considered to be worth a fortune today, can it be any less true for property bought today when considered 100 years from now? Fifty years in the future? Ten?

TIP

Don't be intimidated by price. It's much like clothing. Most people aren't aware that today's formal clothing is really the day-to-day business clothing of the previous generation's. Similarly, most of the prices that we use to judge by are the prices paid yesterday for things. Keep up to date. Higher prices today are, in many cases, simply a reflection of inflation, of the declining buying power of our currency. Don't fall into the trap of believing that prices could never go higher. They always have.

As long as we continue to have inflation and our money continues to be worth less and less, real estate will be worth more and more. As we've seen, it helps if shortages of housing drive prices up, but it really doesn't matter. It helps if there's increased demand from a growing population, but it really doesn't matter. It helps if construction materials cost more, but it really doesn't matter. The only thing that really matters is inflation. As long as there's inflation, housing will increase in value. And it doesn't look as though inflation is going away any time soon. (Two hundred years of inflation can't be wrong.)

CAUTION

There are a number of economists who are predicting we are entering an era of deflation—that is, a time when money will become more valuable, and commodities, including real estate, will cost less. While there was a stronger chance of this before the turn of the century, I haven't seen any recent evidence to support the view. Should it happen, however, it would have an adverse effect on property values.

Cheap Financing

Yet another piece of the background that influences our ability to succeed as residential real estate (RE) investors is financing. Few RE investors pay cash—almost all rely on getting someone else to put up the funds for a purchase. And the one characteristic of the recent housing boom that separated it from all others was the availability of cheap and easy money. That continues on today, though at a much more constrained pace.

Twenty years ago it was considered common to put 20 percent down when you bought a property. Today ten percent down is common.

Twenty years ago interest rates around 10 to 12 percent or higher were common. More recently they've been lower.

The fact of the matter is that it has become much easier to buy real estate using other people's money.

TIP

As an investor, you may still need to put some money down to make a purchase (or use other property you own as collateral). But if you can manage to be both an investor and a homeowner (actually move into the home), then nothing-down financing may be available for you.

The effects of cheap money on real estate investing cannot be minimized. It enables players to enter and pursue the game. It will make it possible for you to get started and succeed.

Where do you get easy financing? How do you secure it? We'll go into the details in later chapters (especially Chapter 20). For now, however, just keep in mind that in the background along with a housing shortage and inflation, there are lenders hovering. They're waiting for good properties and investors to come along, and they are willing to give you money to make your investment purchase.

CAUTION

Real estate is interest rate sensitive. Should interest rates rise, property sales and values could be expected to decline. Interest rate hikes are unlikely to happen unless the economy gets suddenly stronger or there is some unanticipated national or international event (such as an abrupt halt in oil supplies).

A Strong, but Not Too Strong, Economy

Finally, it's important to have a strong economy for the real estate market to prosper, but it doesn't have to be too strong. The real estate recession of the 1990s was triggered by an economic recession. When times are tough and people are out of work, fewer are willing to make big purchases like real estate. And the field suffers.

A healthy economy, on the other hand, is essential for real estate growth. Of course, a good economy makes lenders feel comfortable enough to keep offering great financing.

By the same token, you don't want an economy that's too strong. When the economy builds up a head of steam, there's competition for credit, and easy real estate financing could dry up.

It's important to you as an investor to not only be aware of the first three pieces in the background that will push your success— housing shortage, inflation, and available financing—but also to track the positive or negative effects any changes in the economy could have on the real estate market.

Plan for Success

Finally, there's the matter of having a plan. Yes, the background may tell you that now's a great time to invest in real estate. But how do you do it? What's your plan for success?

We'll examine that in the next chapter.

Hold It or Flip It?

Quit chasing real estate bargains. As long as you're a player in the market, they'll find you.

What could be simpler? You *buy* property . . . You *rent* it out . . . And then you *sell* it.

The devil, as with many things, is in the details.

Do you immediately "flip" the property for a quick profit? Or do you "hold" it for a long term? (And if for a long term, for how long?)

The common wisdom during the last real estate bubble was to flip any piece of property you had. Buy it and sell it quick, even if the profit was small. And then do it again. And again.

That worked for a while because the market was hot, some say superheated. But what about when the market's more normal, going sideways, or even declining? Yes, it's definitely easier in a cooler market to find properties below market that have a potential for flipping and profit taking. But, on the other hand, it's much harder to find buyers who will pay top prices for those properties. As a result, flipping has become a far less realistic alternative than holding properties.

Of course, if you're the type who can sell ice cubes to Eskimos and coal to Newcastlers, I suppose a cooling market is going to be no problem to you. But what if you're more an average person who wants to invest in real estate but doesn't see himself or herself as a clever Donald Trump? Yes, you want the profits, but you aren't an ultra-sophisticated investor. You're willing to work hard, but you worry that you'll make mistakes. You're willing to spend your time, but you're not confident you will come across the big moneymaking deals.

Is there a simpler way for you to invest in real estate?

Yes, of course there is. You can successfully invest by buying and "holding." It's a calmer strategy—buying and holding for the long term. In some cases, buying and holding indefinitely. We'll look into this plan of attack in this chapter, as well as see when and how to flip properties.

Should I Hold Properties for a Very Long Term?

My father was actually the person who taught me this process. He believed in it completely and worked at it his entire life.

The idea is really quite simple. You acquire properties (single-family homes, condos, small strip malls—whatever) slowly, one at a time, over a period of years. You buy, but you seldom sell. Over time you acquire a vast holding in real estate. This is like holding real estate for holding's sake.

Perhaps you know someone who has done this. Typically they lead quiet lives and are not ostentatious. You may have several in your neighborhood. Many have regular jobs, they are successful, and they devote their time to taking care of their properties. They are most busy at the first of the month when they go around "harvesting"—that is, collecting their rents.

You see, over time the mortgages on these properties get paid down. When they are originally purchased, the mortgage may be very high, often 80 to 95 percent of the purchase price. (These investors often live in the properties they buy for a time before converting them to rentals, thus qualifying for a high loan-to-value mortgage.) However, over 30 years that mortgage gets reduced to zero. Now the investor has a paid-off rental, and most of the rent money goes into his or her pocket.

Some investors literally have dozens of such properties that yield high positive cash flows. A few have hundreds. Of course, once that happens, they tend to hire good property management firms to take care of the rentals, and then they retire to a warm climate with sunny beaches.

Should I Keep My Day Job?

Let's make sure we understand the principle: You buy properties and rent them out to make the payments. Eventually you pay them off (or pay them way down) and live off the income they generate.

The plan appeals to many people because of its simplicity. You don't have to be a genius to make it work. You don't have to even work long or, in most cases, hard. Indeed, all you need do is keep your eyes open for good properties and purchase them as you can.

Remember, this is *not* a get-rich-quick scheme. When you start, there will be little to no cash flow from the properties. Instead, you may have to take money out of pocket to pay for maintenance and repairs and occasionally to offset some mortgage and tax payments when the rent's late or a tenant can't pay. Keep your day job!

Of course, you may get some immediate tax relief. Or depending on your income, you may not. It is for this reason that you should plan on continuing to do whatever it is you do for a living.

Additionally many investors begin by moving into their investment house initially. Because it is their principal residence, they can deduct their property taxes and mortgage interest. And they can fix up the property while they stay there. Plus, they get the benefit of low-down financing.

How Do I Cash Out?

As we've seen, over time your mortgage goes down and your rents go up. Your positive cash flow increases, and you pull money out. However, if you need cash, you can always refinance the property. Buy a property and hold it for five years, and chances are it will be worth considerably more than you paid for it. Now you can refinance to get that new equity out.

Buy one property, hold it a few years, get cash out, and buy another home. Now you've got two. Hold them a few years, cash out, and buy two more homes. Now you've got four. Keep repeating the process and it won't be too many years before you yourself are a land baron!

Can Anyone Do It?

When I've first explained the concept of long-term real estate holding, often people have remarked that it's so obvious—why didn't they think of it? Indeed, it is obvious and so simple that almost anyone can do it. However, there are some potential drawbacks that you should be aware of.

The first is that it works best if you start young. Then you have the years to acquire the property. If you start near retirement age, you will still be able to acquire a number of properties, but you will find that you're going to need to nurture these young ventures just when you want to get money out to retire. For those nearing retirement age, a better plan is to buy, rent, and sell as described throughout the rest of this book.

The other concern is that, as we've noted in many places, real estate is cyclical. And if you simply buy and hold indefinitely, you're really not taking advantage of the cycles.

One of the things that I like to do is to sell when prices accelerate and then buy back other properties when prices fall.

Of course, this can be a risky strategy. If you miss the top or the bottom by a large margin, it can be costly. On the other hand, if you guess right, you can clear significant profits on your properties, much more than you could by simply holding on indefinitely.

What Kind of Properties Should I Look For?

Buildings, all buildings, have a limited lifespan. While it may not seem that way at any given point in time, it's a fact. A 25-year-old house may seem perfectly sound today. However, in another 25 years it may be falling down and requiring all sorts of costly repairs. A 50-year-old house may seem like a bargain, after it's fixed up. But what's it going to cost you to maintain it when it's 75 years old!

The key to buying property for the long term is to buy that property when it's young, no more than 10 years old. That way as you grow old gracefully, so will your real estate. Twenty-five years from now, with the proper maintenance, the house should still be in reasonably good shape, and it should still be producing a healthy rental income.

Also, watch out for the neighborhoods. Today's fine blue-collar or white-collar neighborhood may become tomorrow's slum. If you buy long term into a neighborhood that turns sour, you'll own a home in an area where you may eventually be afraid to go and collect the rent!

You need to buy in sound neighborhoods, ones that will remain solid year after year. But how do you identify this type of neighborhood?

Quite frankly, short of having a crystal ball, no one can know for sure what will happen to a neighborhood 25 years down the road. However, some things tend to remain constant. If the neighborhood is near good schools and shopping and it "looks good" with lots of trees and landscaping; if it's away from industry, commercial settings, and heavily trafficked streets; and most important, if it's recognized as a "good neighborhood" when you buy—then chances are it will remain so for a long time to come.

When you're buying short term, you can ignore a neighborhood problem such as a large commercial center or run-down homes a few streets over. But you can't ignore such things when you buy long term.

Where Are the Alligators?

The last thing in the world you want is a bunch of properties that eat at you rather than feed you (called *alligators* in the trade). Since you're going to hold these properties for a very long time, it is crucial that right from the start they be at breakeven or close to it. Buying properties with big negative cash flows is a no-no. You might be able to handle one or even two. But acquire more and you'll simply be overwhelmed by the cash drain.

How do you find properties that will feed you rather than eat at you?

It's simple: *wait* for the right property to show up. The beauty of this plan is that it doesn't require you to take precipitous action. You have a lifetime to buy your properties. As long as you're always out there looking, sooner or later you'll come across a suitable deal. It may take several months. In a tight market, it could even take a year or more. But it will happen. When you see a good deal (a breakeven property), acquire it.

What If I Can Flip It?

That, of course, is where most people feel the action is. Flipping gets you cash out of the property—and fast. My suggestion is that whenever possible, you *do* flip a property. However, don't push it. Don't try to flip a property when it won't budge, or when the market's not right.

TIP

Flipping is different from buying, renting out for a time, and then selling (which we'll discuss in the remainder of this book). When you flip, you rarely hold the property more than a few months. When you buy, rent, and then sell, you usually hold it for a few years.

Here's a quick course on flipping:

Rules for Flipping

1. **Buy right.** You can flip only if you buy at a low price.
2. **Don't take the title.** If possible, you don't want to own the property—the transaction costs will overwhelm you.
3. **Have a buyer waiting in the wings.** These are fast deals; you don't have time to go looking for a buyer.
4. **Provide full disclosure.** The way to avoid trouble in these deals is to make sure everyone knows everything.

How Can I Flip in a Cold Market?

When the market slows down, it's harder to flip. As noted, it's much easier in a cold market to find bargain properties. However, it's harder to find *rebuyers* (the next buyer who purchases through you) who are willing to move quickly. The reason is that when the market slows down, buyers become more cautious. They want to see that they are getting a bargain. Therefore, in order to flip, you have to reduce your profit and give the buyer a good reason to purchase quickly.

The mechanics of the deal are fairly straightforward. Once you locate a suitable property, you present your offer. If the seller accepts, you have a period of time in which to resell. Depending on how that offer was structured (as an "option" or an "assignment," to be explained later), your time period can be anywhere from a minimum of about 30 days to a maximum of about six months.

You then bring in a rebuyer (one who actually purchases the property) who concludes the sale with the original seller. The cash transfer is done in escrow. The new buyer gets a mortgage and puts up a cash down payment in the usual fashion. A portion of the purchase price goes to cash out the original seller. And you get the remainder, usually in cash, but sometimes in the form of a second mortgage, for yourself.

When Is It Not Really Flipping?

Note, the way we've defined *flipping* here, it involves not actually taking the title to the property. Some investors, however, prefer to take the title, hold the property for a period of time, say, six months, and then resell it.

The problem with doing this lies in the transaction costs. Assuming you use an agent, the typical transaction costs (escrow, title insurance, loan fees, commission, and so on) in a real estate round-trip (buying and selling) are 10 percent of the final price. That means that the property has to appreciate 10 percent before you can break even. While that kind of appreciation was certainly the case during the early years of this century, it's not the usual case in more normal times. Indeed, 5 percent per year has been historically the typical rate of appreciation. Thus, if you buy and hold for 6 months and then try to resell (5 percent appreciation versus 10 percent transaction costs), you'll lose money. The transaction costs will eat up your money.

The exception, of course, would be if you were to find a bargain that you could buy for significantly below market price. But if that's the case, why bother to go through with a full purchase? Why not use an option or an assignment to gain control of the property without taking the title?

But what is an option, and what is an assignment?

These are two techniques that savvy investors use when flipping properties. They're fairly sophisticated techniques, so we'll take an entire chapter (18) to explain them in detail.

So Should I Hold It or Flip It?

So, should you hold property for the long term or flip it?

The answer is determined by the deal. Flip when you can; hold when you can't.

Buying

Eleven Steps to Finding Good Properties in Any Market

If it's not a bargain, a steal, or a terrific deal, pass. There are 8 million properties sold each year in the United States, and there's no reason you should invest in a mediocre one.

The dream of acquiring wealth is as old as America itself. While some of the original settlers came to this country to avoid religious persecution, most, particularly the later immigrants, came not only to acquire freedom but also to get rich.

That combined dream of freedom and acquiring wealth has played out through the history of the country. John Jacob Astor built his wealth in New York City by acquiring real estate ahead of growth, waiting for the city to catch up and selling for profit. The railroad barons acquired wealth not by bridging the continent with trains but by acquiring vast real estate alongside the railroad right-of-way. The majority of today's wealthy, whether they acquired their assets through stock investment or business entrepreneurship, hold much (if not most) of that wealth in the form of real estate.

In short, if you aspire to make your fortune in real estate, you're not alone. You're part of a strong national tradition. And chances are you'll succeed! The number of Americans today who own big stakes real estate is in the many millions.

Of course, the best way to start is by buying one property at a time. And the key is finding the right properties. Here are 11 steps to get you on the correct track.

Step 1. Buy Close to Home

I like to think that after a great many years in real estate, I've made all of the mistakes. Buying too far from home is one of the worst mistakes—fortunately, I made it early on and didn't repeat it.

Never buy far from home if you're going to rent out the property. If you do, I can almost guarantee you'll regret it. (By the way, this doesn't apply if you're going to flip a property—you can buy that anywhere. Just be sure it is, in fact, flippable—see the previous chapter.)

When you invest in real estate as a small investor, you are directly involved in management. You are the person who has to solve the day-to-day problems.

If you're far away, even small tasks can mushroom into big problems. A leaky faucet means an expensive call to a plumber. A broken window, an electrical plug that doesn't work, a fallen shutter, or a lawn that needs mowing—you name it—all require calls to professionals to be called in, if you live at a distance.

If there are big problems, such as tenants who won't pay, then you must fly or drive miles to solve them (or hire an expensive property management company to do it for you).

But if you're close by, you can put a for-rent ad in the local paper and from that point on, do it all yourself. If a tenant doesn't pay, you can be right there and talk with the tenant to find out what the problem is and correct it. If there's plumbing, gardening, electrical, or other small work to be done, you can do it yourself or find a close-by handyman to help with it.

In short, when it's vitally important to be right on the spot when you have a real estate problem, if you live close, it's no problem.

I have a real estate attorney friend who handles hundreds of units. He gave me the only exception to the above rule. It's this: If you have 20 units or more, then you can handle it as an absentee landlord. With that many units as a minimum, you can afford to hire a good manager who will take good care of your properties. With fewer than 20 units, however, you can't afford a manager. Consequently, you need to do it yourself.

It's important not to get the wrong message here, however. I'm not saying that rental real estate is a really tough investment. It's not: 95 percent of all problems can be handled in just a few minutes, if you care enough to do it right. If you're there, you can pick the right tenants. You can do minor work yourself. You can hire out major work to people you know and can get recommendations on.

In short, being there makes the difference. After my own first mistake in buying property a state away, I have since rented many other properties for dozens of years and have never come across a problem I couldn't quickly and easily handle myself.

Step 2. Don't Pay Market Price

When you make your final decision to purchase a property, make sure the price you pay for it is below the market price. If you pay full market price or more, you'll lose when it comes time to resell. Remember, you make your profit when you buy, not when you sell. As an investor, you need to think about buying properties "wholesale" and then reselling retail.

Of course, determining whether a price is below market can be difficult when prices are rising or falling. However, checking the comparable sales for the area can be a big help.

Typically there are other recent sales of homes similar to the one that you are considering buying. You can look at those comparables to see what price such houses have recently been selling for, to get an idea what your subject house is worth.

Get an agent to do a free *comparative market analysis* (CMA). It will show all comps with their list and sales prices and features, as well as other useful information. A CMA is very helpful when you're trying to determine value. Also, check www.dataquick.com and www.zillow.com.

The real trick is trying to decide how much the market adds to or subtracts from the value of the home in question. My suggestion is to play the percentages. If property values are changing 6 percent a year and it's been four months since the last comparable was sold, add or subtract about 2 percent (one-third of a year's increase) for appreciation or depreciation. That's just a rule of thumb, but it ought to get you pretty close to the current market value of the property.

You can determine how hot or cold the market is by checking with local brokers and even the local newspapers. They are always giving out the statistics for overall price appreciation in the area, particularly when it's on the way up.

Once you know what the market value is, insist on paying less. Check Step 10 for tips on how to do just that.

Step 3. Buy Single-Family Residential Homes (to Start)

I like houses best, even over condos, for these reasons: They are easy to buy (financing is readily available). They are easy to rent (most people prefer them to any other type of housing). They are comparatively easy to maintain. And when it comes time to resell, you usually get the highest profits.

Don't listen to so-called professional investors who knock the single-family home as an investment. I have heard those who can afford to buy 100-unit apartment buildings disparage the house as an investment property. They might say, "If I have a 100-unit building and I have one vacancy, it's only 1 percent of my income that I'm losing. But if I have a single-family house and I have one vacancy, I lose 100 percent of my income. There's no way to justify that!"

Baloney! If you have one unit and find one tenant, you have 100 percent occupancy. If you have a 100-unit apartment, you have to find 100 tenants to get full occupancy.

Either way, it's just a war of words. What counts are results. I've been renting single-family housing for more than 30 years in good markets and bad, and as long as I've been doing it personally, I've never had serious trouble finding a tenant. And I've always sold for a profit. My feeling is that if you're new to investment real estate, the best place to start is with a single-family house.

As a general rule, beware of condos as an investment. The temptation to buy may prove nearly irresistible because they are typically offered at lower prices than houses. But when you look at those low prices, you have to keep in mind that historically, in a down market they fall first in value and go lower. Further, condos may often rent for only 70 to 80 percent of the rate of a comparably sized single-family home. It may seem very appealing to buy a lower-cost condo, but you'll find them harder to rent and harder to sell.

Also, don't overlook the hidden costs of condominium ownership, mainly homeowners association (HOA) fees. These can often add hundreds of dollars a month to your payments.

Duplexes, triplexes, flats, and so on often make good investments especially if they are located in an area of mainly single-family homes. You can sometimes buy them relatively cheaply (when compared to single-family homes) and rent them for most, if not all, of your payment. Upon resale, they tend to hold up well. Best of all, unlike condos, they tend to have no HOA fees.

But beware of trying to combine home and investment here. Many people buy a duplex or triplex thinking they will rent out one or two units to help offset costs while living in the remaining unit. The thought is that you have both a home and an investment property. The reality is that you end up with the worst of both possible worlds. You don't really have a home because your tenant is right next door. (He or she will be over every other minute with complaints.) In addition, you don't really have a good rental because you're not able to offer a single-family detached home that can command top dollar.

Co-ops can be great to live in, but impossible rentals. The board often will be on your back if you try to rent out the property. They may want to approve every tenant, holding up the rental process. Additionally, some co-ops may try to restrict your ability to rent your property at all.

Small apartment buildings are a mixed bag for the investor. Mainly it's a matter of management. You will find that you have far more tenant movement here. If you have four houses, chances are you might change only one or two tenants during a year. With a four-unit apartment building, you might change as many as four or more tenants during that same time frame! Managing an apartment building is double or triple the work of managing the same number of single-family housing units.

My suggestion is that until you've handled a few rental houses, hold up on tackling even a small apartment building.

On the other hand, profits upon selling can be enormous. The value of apartment buildings is directly related to their rental income. The higher the rental income, the greater the value. The surest way to make money in real estate is to buy an apartment building, jack up the rents, and then resell. Typically for each dollar you increase your annual rental income, you could get between $6 and

$12 in profit on the sale. If you have four units and raise the rent $100 on each, that means an extra $400 a month, or $4,800 a year, times a multiple of, for example, 10, meaning an instant profit of $48,000—all on a modest $100-a-month rent increase. (Beware, however, of rent control areas where it is impossible to increase rental rates.)

Step 4. Look in Better (but Not the Best) Neighborhoods

The better the neighborhood, the easier it will be to rent and eventually to sell (or trade) your property. Homes in good neighborhoods are always in demand, while those in poor neighborhoods languish. On the other hand, don't try for the very best areas. They are often overpriced, and it will be difficult for you to find an investment property there that will rent for enough to cover your monthly costs.

What makes a good neighborhood? Look for attractive homes; avoid areas where landscaping is neglected. Look for wide streets; avoid areas where abandoned cars litter streets. Look for conformity in housing; avoid areas where there is a hodge-podge of homes.

Especially, check the schools. The most reliable indicator of a good neighborhood is that it has high-quality schools, as evidenced by high scores on standardized tests (always available at the main school district office or online). Poor school scores too often mean a neighborhood with poor price appreciation.

Step 5. Always Look First for Flippable Properties

The term *flipping* has come into the real estate vernacular along with the big boom in property values. It essentially means that you quickly buy and then resell a property without holding onto it. If you can flip a property and make a profit on it, the reasoning goes, do it.

I agree, up to a point. The cash generated by flipping can go toward your own income (supporting yourself) as well as toward creating capital for the down payment on another property. Flipping, when possible, has always been a good way to generate cash from real estate.

The mistake that some people make, however, is to look *only* for flippable properties, or to try and flip properties that really aren't suitable. It makes little sense to flip a property to make $10,000 when if you held it for a couple of years, you could make $100,000. Also, out of 25 properties you look at, you'll be lucky to find one that's truly flippable. Yet, 5 of the others might be good for holding, renting, and then reselling.

Remember, building long-term wealth involves holding and renting a majority of your real estate.

Step 6. Look Where Tenant Markets Are Strongest

It's a truism that there are always tenants. But the underlying fact is that in some locales, there are more tenants than in others. And in some locales, the tenant population can afford to pay a higher rent than can the tenant population in other areas. Ideally, you want to buy in an area where there are lots of high-income tenants with the ability to pay higher rents.

It's important here to think locally. The country may be doing well or poorly economically, but your own area may be doing better, or worse, than the nation as a whole.

How well is your particular area doing? Remember, in order to get a tenant for your property, you must be able to draw on local workers. If there are few well-paying local jobs, you won't get many good tenants.

As a consequence, it's important to do a tenant analysis before leaping ahead and buying rental property. There are a variety of ways to accomplish this: First, if you're buying into low-income housing, look for blue-collar tenants. That usually means some sort of industry nearby. On the other hand, if you're buying an upscale property, look for white-collar workers. Check for office buildings, commercial buildings, financial institutions, and the like in your area.

Second, think like a tenant. If you're a tenant, who's going to employ you? Look around your area. Who are the big employers? Find the place that the tenant wants to live and that's where you'll have your strongest tenant market.

Third, check the local newspapers under "homes for rent." You'll quickly see which areas have rentals. Call to see what the prices are (if they aren't listed). Then recheck the same paper over several weeks. If you find areas that have the same homes advertised for weeks on end, try to avoid those. If there are areas where homes rarely crop up and the ads for them appear only for a single weekend, go there. That's likely the area where the tenants want to live. Areas that rent quickly indicate a good rental market. Areas with lots of vacancies do not.

Finally, check with brokers and rental agencies. Often in a single conversation they can give you as much information as you could collect in weeks of personally conducting your own investigations. (It's a good idea to do some personal legwork anyway, just to be sure that what you are being told is, in fact, accurate.)

Step 7. Buy Properties with Positive Cash Flow

Your basic strategy is to buy and rent out property until you can sell for a hefty profit. But in order to hold that property, you have to be able to rent it for enough money to pay your expenses.

Can you realistically do that?

You can *if* the property produces a positive cash flow. That means that the income from rents exceeds (or at least breaks even with) the expenses of ownership (including financing, taxes, and insurance).

Can you find rental property that will cover all your expenses? In truth, today it's often difficult to do. However, it's not impossible, particularly after taking into consideration the tax benefits of ownership.

However, observing the rule that you should look before leaping, I always check the price-to-rent ratio on any property *before* buying it. That way I avoid surprises. Some properties seem like they should be able to carry themselves, or close to it, but an analysis reveals that they are instead alligators. (Their expenses eat up their rental income, and you have to feed them from your own pocket.) Buy without checking this ratio, and you're at risk.

The price-to-rent ratio is simply a rule of thumb that wise investors use to gauge the relationship between monthly rental income, the monthly expenses, and the price of the property. It simply says that the monthly income from rents should be around 0.7 to 1 percent of the total purchase price (depending on such factors as interest and tax rates). If the monthly rent is less than 0.7 percent, unless the property is flippable, it might be just too expensive. Here's how to make the calculation:

$$\frac{\text{Monthly rent}}{\text{Purchase price}} = \text{Price-to-rent ratio}$$

$$\frac{\$\,3{,}500}{\$\,500{,}000} = .007, \text{ or } 0.7 \text{ percent}$$

If your property has a value of $200,000, then 1 percent is simply $2,000. If it can't generate around $1,400 to $2,000 in rent, you probably won't be able to cover all your expenses. If your property's value is $500,000, it should be able to generate around $3,500+. This should result in your not having to take money (possibly a lot of money) out of your own pocket each month just to hang onto the property. No one wants to do that, certainly not for any extended period of time.

Note: We haven't taken into account any tax advantages that you might be able to get, such as depreciation. This may or may not be available to you.

TRAP

If you e-mail me saying that you can't find property that fits this ratio, my answer will be, "look harder." With rents going up and prices going down in recent years, this rule of thumb continues to work. Some investors, however, want to stretch it. They can't find positive cash flow properties, so they look for ones with negative cash flow. My advice is to pull back. Unless you can easily cover the negative (the "alligator" effect), don't get involved. Over time a negative cash flow property will too easily pull you down.

Step 8. Look for Low-Expense Properties

Knowing your true rental expenses is very important. You can't know whether the property will float until and unless you know what your real expenses are.

Typical Basic Rental Expenses: PITI

Principal and Interest (the mortgage payments)
Taxes
Insurance

These amounts are the easiest to determine. Just contact a mortgage broker to find the first. Give him or her the amount of your mortgage, and you'll quickly get the monthly payment for principal and interest.

Any real estate agent can give you a pretty good idea of how much your property taxes will be. And an insurance agent can very quickly give you a ballpark figure for your fire and liability insurance. (Yes, with rentals you definitely also will need liability insurance.)

The remainder of your expenses is variable. By the way, "variable" does not mean that you may or may not incur them. It means that while they will definitely be there, the amounts will vary month to month and year to year.

Maintenance

The biggest unknown factor is maintenance. You won't know what's going to break until it does. However, you can pretty much guess that the older the property, the more maintenance it will require. Here's a rule of thumb for maintenance costs on rental property:

Maintenance Costs versus Age of Property

AGE OF PROPERTY, YEARS	MAINTENANCE AS A PERCENTAGE OF MONTHLY INCOME
0–10	0–5%
10–25	10%
25–older	15–20%

As you can see, the allowance for maintenance goes up with the age of the property. As a result, for investment I suggest you always try to buy younger properties. You'll save a fortune on maintenance costs.

Vacancies

Then there are vacancies. No property is rented all of the time. If you're a good landlord and on top of things, however, your property can be rented almost all the time. A fairly reliable rule of thumb for you to use if you are a good landlord is that the property will be vacant at least two weeks out of each year, assuming you've picked a strong rental market and you actively participate in getting tenants.

Other Costs

Of course, there are yet other costs. You will want to figure what your time is worth managing the property (or calculate the cost of hiring professional management). And then there may be costs of fix-up if the property is run down when you purchase it. We'll look at some of these in Chapter 9. Some people accurately figure the PITI, but then they overlook all the other costs simply because it's so hard to find a rental property that makes enough income to cover them. Nevertheless, it's better to spend more time looking than buy a bad property and keep taking money out of your pocket every month.

Step 9. Insist on Favorable Terms

Sellers are often hung up on price. They may be convinced that lowering the price is the absolutely last resort.

If that's the case, don't try moving a stone wall. Go around it. Offer the seller the price he or she wants, but insist on favorable terms.

For example, at the price asked, it may be impossible to buy the property, rent it out, and break even monthly. (In this case, the ratio noted above simply doesn't work out.) However, the sellers may have a large equity in the property. So instead of getting a new mortgage from an institutional lender, you demand that the sellers themselves carry back a mortgage at 5 percent instead of the then going rate of 7 percent. Suddenly your mortgage payments are cut. Now the price-to-rent ratio falls into line.

If the sellers protest, you can point out that you're paying full price. Many sellers, being penny wise and pound foolish, will go along.

Terms are critical. Often you can give the seller his or her price and still get a bargain by negotiating for more favorable terms for yourself.

Step 10. Always Lowball the Seller

My suggestion is that as an investor, you always lowball sellers. This means offering way below what they are asking. How far below? An offer that is 5 to 10 percent below asking price is not unreasonable for an investor. Offers of as much as 25 to 30 percent below asking price are uncommon, but not unheard of.

If you think that lowballing seldom works, you are making a big mistake. While it's definitely hard in a hot market, and you'll certainly have to raise the amount you offer, in a cold market where sellers are desperate, it's more likely to succeed than you might think.

Lowballing is a technique that some investors have worked out to perfection. It requires two elements: persistence and guts.

The persistence is required because you won't get a seller to accept every time, or every other time, or even most times. You have to be willing to make offers that get turned down time and again. You have to be willing to keep on trying until you finally hit the right seller.

TRAP

It's a big mistake to fall in love with an investment house. An investment house is strictly a business proposition. One house is as good as another, and you simply want one that will meet your financial and economic criteria. Never mind the cute archway in the living room or the adorable French windows. The questions you need to ask have to do with price, terms, rentability, and ultimate resale. Leave your heart home when buying investment property. Bring only your head.

"Guts" come in because you have to be willing to accept a lot of criticism. Real estate brokers will criticize your actions. (This is only natural because, in most cases, they represent the sellers and they don't get paid a commission unless there's a sale. They don't like making lots of unsuccessful offers.)

You also have to have the courage to try and try again even after many offers are rejected. Remember, every dollar below market that you buy a property for is a dollar of profit in your pocket.

Never be sympathetic to the seller who wants more money. Helping a seller to make more money on the sale may be a generous, altruistic act. But it really doesn't make good business sense.

Step 11. Start by Converting Your Own Home to a Rental

Most people sell their current house when they buy another. They own only one home at a time. But if your investment goal is to come up with an investment property, why not convert your existing home to a rental and then buy your next home to live in?

Keep in mind that you must want to sell your present home for this scenario to work. After all, you've got to live somewhere. However, if this is something that's already in the works, then consider how a conversion could offer benefits.

There are all sorts of good reasons for doing a conversion. The biggest, however, is that you already know the property and own it. You don't have to go through the process of finding, investigating, and buying. It's a done deal right away. All you need do is look for a new home to live in.

But many owners will immediately protest: "I need the equity from my current home in order to buy my next one."

Are you sure of that?

You may be able to swing the deal with little financial strain, if you know how. We'll look into equity conversion in Chapter 19. But first, determine if your current home will make a good rental property.

Is Your Home Suitable to Be a Rental? Not all properties are. Some simply require too much loving tender care. These are typically homes with extensive landscaping, with white carpeting, with delicate nooks and crannies . . . a high-maintenance property. If you have one of these, you're probably better off selling. The home needs the care of an owner, which is not something a tenant will provide. Other considerations are these:

1. **Is your home in a good rental area?** Some areas are near large employers, and for that reason, they have a ready-made rental base. Others are in the remote suburbs where there are almost exclusively homeowners rather than renters. Check out the rental market in your area. Look in the local newspapers. Are there lots of rentals? If so, do they rent up quickly? Call a few landlords and a few agents to find out.

2. **Do you have rules restricting rentals?** Some properties belong to HOAs (homeowners associations) or boards that want to have the right to approve tenants. This is particularly the case with co-ops. Some single-family homes are in an HOA (often a gated community), and the boards show their disdain of rental properties by continually fining owners-landlords for rule infractions. If you've got an HOA or a board to contend with, it's worth taking a little time to find out just what its policy is toward rentals.

3. **Can you make more by selling outright?** Sometimes it makes more sense to sell than to rent. If you're at the peak of the market cycle, you might want to get out while the getting is good. On the other hand, if you anticipate much higher prices in the future, you're far better off to hold for a time.

If your home passes muster, then by all means consider converting it to a rental and holding it long enough to get a better price. You'll become an instant investor!

There you have 11 steps to finding just the right property for you. So what are you waiting for? Get started!

Identifying Breakout Bargains

I always look to see if other properties have turned around because if you're the first to buy in a turnaround neighborhood, you're sure to get hammered.

Not all properties appreciate in price at the same rate. Some go up much faster than others. Buy one of the properties that are appreciating faster and you'll profit more and quicker.

Los Angeles: A Case Study

There were people who made a killing in the real estate market a few years ago in Los Angeles, California. It wasn't so much that they happened to be in the right place at the right time but that they took advantage of a situation as it developed.

Back at the turn of the century, the country, and in particular southern California, was just coming out of the worst real estate recession since the Great Depression. (This was before the huge "bubble" that saw prices skyrocket around the country.) Property prices had declined roughly 15 to 25 percent during the previous seven years. There were those who said that the price of property would continue to go down, almost indefinitely. Of course, anyone with common sense knew that was simply nonsense.

Those who realized that prices had bottomed out began buying up property, mainly single-family homes in higher-priced areas.

TIP

When prices turn up, it's often felt first in the premium properties, those at the top end of the spectrum. Then it works its way down to medium- and the modest-priced properties.

In well-known areas such as Palos Verdes, Malibu, the West Side, and others, investors were buying up luxury homes in the $500,000 to $700,000 price range. Some were as low as $400,000. (That may not seem inexpensive compared to other areas of the country, but for the areas in question, it was bargain basement time.)

These investors then rented out these homes to make their payments. They simply sat on them and waited for times to change.

And change they did. Within two years, most of the luxury areas of Los Angeles made up all of the price declines and moved ahead of their previous all-time highs. Within a year or two, in fact, many of the original investors were looking at price appreciations ranging from 100 to 300 percent! This was at the same time that the prices of many more modestly priced properties had not yet risen to their previous highs before the real estate recession.

Of course, afterward most of the country climbed aboard the bandwagon. Further, the price increases were no longer limited to luxury properties. They were up and down the spectrum from moderate units to the least expensive properties.

Finding the Turnaround Area

Of course, not all areas saw huge prices increases. Parts of the South and Midwest saw only modest price increases. And since then, prices have turned downward along both coasts.

However, that doesn't mean that new opportunities don't abound. It would be a mistake to think that turnaround areas are only regional by nature. Within any given city at any given time, there may be some neighborhoods that are shooting up in price, others that are simply moseying along at the same price, and others that are going down. The real question becomes, how do you identify the next area to see rapid price increases near where you live?

Here are five indicators that suggest where and when an area is about to take off.

Price-Rise Indicators

1. Growth is currently slower than it is in other areas nearby.
2. There is a higher volume of resales.
3. There is new development coming.
4. There is noticeable growth in business development areas.
5. Prices have started turning around.

Currently Slow Growth

A slow growth area may be ripe for a turnaround. Or not. A lot depends on factors totally out of the control of the local residents. For example, parts of some eastern cities (such as Detroit or Newark) that saw blighted areas for many years have been the target of renovation funds from government and private industry. This money, coupled with new jobs caused by a healthy economy, has caused some neighborhoods in these areas to turn around, which has created real estate investment opportunities.

The key, of course, is to find an area in its early turnaround phase, and then buy it and hold. Within a few years, residential property values should increase.

A new key factor is *close-in location*. Between the 1950s and the 1990s America expanded with new highways leading people to ever farther away neighborhoods. However, as the population has increased, the infrastructure of roads has become antiquated, unable to maintain the pace set by commuters. In Los Angeles, for example, the expected average speed on the "free"-ways is anticipated to soon drop to under 10 miles per hour. People who used to commute between Stockton, California, and the Silicon Valley (roughly an 80-mile ride) may soon find the ride could take up to four hours or more each way.

In short, those old neighborhoods close to downtown that people abandoned only a few years ago are suddenly looking a whole lot better. People tired of fighting an impossible commute are coming back. All of which means that close-in properties are once again in fashion and are jumping up in value. Why not take advantage of it?

High Resale Volume

Regardless of what we just discussed, you don't want to be on the "bleeding edge" of the curve. You don't want to jump into a neighborhood that won't be renovated for 10 years. You want one that's already in the process of turning around.

How can you tell the difference?

Look closely. In older areas of cities that are undergoing renovation, you'll see many buildings being refurbished. Indeed, in these areas a carpenter can be that hardest thing to find.

A more precise indicator would be the recent sales figures for local residential properties. What you want to see is a sudden hike in the *number* of sales. That indicates that the area has been "discovered" and investors and owners are pouring in.

TRAP

It's just as bad to be too early as too late. As people discover a new (old) area of town and pour in, the existing inventory of homes gets used up. This process can take anywhere from a few months to several years. While the unsold inventory exists, prices will remain stable. But as soon as that old inventory is gone, price jumps will occur. You want to get in while that old inventory is still available. But move too soon and the distress of the neighborhood (blight, vandalism, drugs, and so on) can do in the best of intentions.

New Developments

Brand-new housing is sometimes a bargain. Buy it from the builder and just rent and hold it. Within a few years it could accelerate in value.

Of course, not all new housing will rise rapidly in price. Generally speaking, you want new developments that are near major employers to ensure a steady supply of employed renters and buyers. Also, any new development in an already established area (such as the last land available for residential construction in a small city) is usually a good buy.

One way to tell if your judgment is right is to look at the competition for the housing. If there are buyers waiting in line to buy the new homes before they're even built, it's a good bet that it's a tract that will shoot up in value. But if there are dozens of already built homes sitting idly waiting for buyers, reconsider. There may be some fatal flaw in the area that will keep it from going up in value. (In Phoenix, for example, for years recently built tracts languished because land was so cheap that even newer tracts nearby quickly came on line. These newer homes flooded the market making it impossible to resell one of the older homes.)

Areas Slated for Growth

John Jacob Astor's plan for making millions in New York City was simple: Just buy property in the area into which the city is growing (at that time being in the direction of the dairy farms) and wait for the growth to reach you. When it does, sell for millions. And he did.

You can do the same thing. Only be *careful*. Growth has an annoying habit of changing directions. A city seems to be growing in one direction, only to reverse and go to the other side of town.

One thing you can watch for is large open space. New growth requires bigger stores, parking, and housing. That means *lots* of land. Generally speaking in today's world, you can go into almost any city and see which area offers the widest open space (even if there is no current development there), and within a few years, that's where everyone will want to be.

Be like Astor, and you can make millions too.

Recent Increases in the Prices of Listed Properties

Finally there's the lazy person's way to find neighborhoods that will boom. Simply watch the price changes.

No, it's not simpleminded. Local real estate boards, newspapers, and various Internet services (such as www.dataquick.com or www.zillow.com) will frequently list price increases by city and sometimes, by neighborhood. Track them.

If you're among the first to realize that one particular area is suddenly showing signs of rapid price increase, go there and check it out. You may find that it's a boomtown in the making. And all you'll need do is buy a house or two to participate.

TIP

Remember, you don't have to be the first to buy a house in a booming area, just as you don't have to pick the bottom of the stock market, to win. You just have to be one of the crowd who rides the wave to the top.

Don't worry over buying wrong. Almost every area eventually goes up in value. You just want to be in those areas that do it sooner and faster.

Getting the Seller to Work for You

Mark Twain once said, "There ought to be a room in every house to swear in."

After reading how far prices have advanced in recent years, most sellers still have dollar signs dancing in their heads. Unfortunately, many simply do not take the reality of today's slower market into account. They truly believe that their house is worth whatever the highest price that a neighbor got for his or her house, even if that sale was years ago at the peak of the market.

Don't cater to the seller's false beliefs. Half the battle in finding good investment property is judging the seller. In today's market you not only have to know what the realistic price is for a property, you also have to find a seller who is motivated enough to accept that price.

Thus, in order for you to get a bargain price, you need to find a seller who is forced to look at prices as they are, not as they were . . . or will be.

The six triggers listed below are some of the factors that might motivate a seller to give you a good price.

Reasons That Motivate a Seller

1. The seller has a job change to a different area necessitating a rapid move.
2. The seller has bought another home and has to quickly sell this one in order to close the deal on the next.
3. The seller has lost his or her job or for other reasons is in financial difficulty and needs to get out, quick.
4. The seller wants to "move up" to a bigger house or to a better area. (This is usually a low motivation.)
5. The seller has some other problem such as a divorce and simply must get rid of the house immediately.
6. For one reason or another, the seller can't make the payments on the property and must sell soon or lose it.

TIP

The highest motivation involves speed. The more quickly a seller must act, the more motivated he or she will be.

In each of the above cases the seller must get out. As a result, he or she will be more willing to accept a realistic price (or offer better terms) because of that motivation. However, unless the seller has one of the above motivations (or one of similar intensity), your chances of getting the house at a good price may be just about nil. Without motivation the seller will simply sit and wait for a better buyer (read one who offers more money) to come by.

Discovering Why a Seller Wants to Make a Move

How do you find out what the seller's motivation really is? Most sellers believe it is a cardinal rule in selling real estate that the seller should always keep up the best front. That's the way to get the best price. Sellers think that if they let a potential buyer know they are highly motivated, they will get a lower offer. So how do you, as a buyer, find out which sellers are, in fact, highly motivated?

The answer is simple. Motivated sellers always tell you they are motivated.

Why would sellers break the cardinal rule? The reason is that highly motivated sellers want out, now. They realize that it's no longer a matter of waiting to get the best price; they just want to sell.

Most very soon realize that keeping quiet about their need to get out quickly won't do the trick anymore. The only way they can get out is if they let every potential buyer—that is, everyone who is even remotely a potential buyer—know their situation.

As a result, it's not a secret. If the house is listed, ask the real estate broker. A highly motivated seller will instruct the broker, "Find any buyer. Tell him or her that I'm highly motivated! Get me any offer!"

Ask the Broker

The real estate broker will move on these words. Any agent worth his or her salt knows that a motivated seller means a quick sale. The broker will alert every potential buyer, including you, that this seller wants out.

Consequently, your first source of motivated sellers is the real estate broker.

But won't the broker buy the property if he or she knows the seller is highly motivated?

You shouldn't worry about this because there's nothing you can do about it. My experience has been that most agents would rather get a commission than buy an investment property. They'll buy investment property only when they can't find a buyer for it.

The exception to this is flippable property. If the agent feels he or she can buy the property and quickly resell for a big profit, he or she may do it. However, agents have special problems in flipping. If they buy themselves and then quickly resell for a profit, the seller may feel cheated and believe that the agent wasn't fulfilling his or her fiduciary relationship. And that seller can do nasty things such as calling the state regulatory board or even taking legal action.

If the agent is foolhardy enough to "double escrow" the property (in essence, sell it before fully taking ownership without letting the seller know what's happening), it might even be illegal. And few agents would dare face the consequences of such action.

Therefore, while it is true that agents will sometimes pick the cream of the crop, there are usually still plenty of good properties out there to go around.

Ask the Seller

Remember, a good way to find out a seller's motivation is to point blank ask the seller. You can do this in a friendly fashion while you tour the house. It's really quite simple. Very frequently when you look at a house, the seller will be there. Just begin a conversation and ask why that seller wants to sell.

If the seller hedges or gives a reason that is not indicative of strong motivation, pass. On the other hand, as noted earlier, the motivated seller is very likely to simply let you know that he or she is extremely eager to get a deal. The seller may say something like, "Make me an offer." Or "Let's talk. If you're interested, put it in writing. I'm very anxious to get out of here." The motivated seller will seldom try to hide his or her eagerness. Rather, he or she will do everything to let you know just how he or she feels.

Ask the Neighbors

Oftentimes neighbors are an excellent source of information. And neighbors may feel little loyalty to the existing owner who is selling and leaving the neighborhood.

Of course, this is not an invitation to be a snoop or to invade anyone's privacy. However, I always suggest that anyone who is interested in buying a property talk to the neighbors about the seller's motivation. (Besides, in the process you may discover there's a bad neighbor next door, which is much better to learn before you buy instead of after.) As part of your general conversation with the neighbor in which you say you're a potential buyer, you will certainly ask about the house and the neighborhood, and eventually the conversation will drift over to the seller. The neighbor may volunteer some critical information as to why the seller is getting out.

Motivated Sellers in Foreclosure

Thus far, we've been assuming that we will find motivated sellers who have their homes listed for sale. But what about sellers who haven't been able to sell their homes for one reason or another and are now in foreclosure? They are the most motivated of all to sell, and they, on occasion, may be able to present some terrific bargain opportunities to you. We'll discuss these in more detail in Chapter 7.

Getting the Bargain

How do you get that bargain once you've discovered a motivated seller?

It's simple: You begin by lowballing (Chapter 6) and then you stick to your guns. The key here is that you now know that your seller is desperate to move the property. Suddenly your own strategy clicks into place. You can afford to be hard-nosed. At every turn, you refuse to knuckle under to the seller's demands. Instead, you make the demands. From an ego standpoint, it's a wonderful position to be in.

A word of caution, however: In a strong market even a highly motivated seller isn't going to be willing to cave into your every demand. The seller will know that if you don't buy this property, another buyer will likely come along shortly. Thus, you would be wise to make your demands reasonable.

In a slow market, however, anything is possible.

Making Lowball Offers That Stick

Every day you're in real estate, you'll have a chance to move outside your comfort zone. Just remember that it's by taking risks that you learn and move up to better deals.

Try never to pay the asking price.

Sellers almost universally are willing to come down in their price. It's up to you as an investor to determine what their lowest point is. If you pay up front what the seller is asking, chances are you're wasting money.

Remember, the less you pay for the property, the greater your profit when you sell.

The real trick is to know how much less than the asking price a seller will take. Sometimes a seller will come down only a few thousand dollars. Other times he or she may drop 10 percent or more. And, of course, there's that occasional seller who refuses to come down a dime. How do you know one from the other?

Unless you've got supernatural powers (or the seller's agent spills the beans), you won't know. That means you have to learn, and one way to do that is through the negotiating process. The seller's reaction to your offer and each counteroffer the seller makes tells you more. Eventually, if you're a good negotiator, you'll get a good price.

The Initial Lowball Offer

It all starts out with a low bid. (You can't very well make a lower bid after you've previously made a higher bid; you would lose credibility and the seller's interest.)

My own rule of thumb is to always offer at least 5 percent less than the asking price for investment homes. Notice, I said "at least." That means that you won't offer less than 5 percent below market, but you might well want to offer far more.

How much more depends on several factors including these:

The market. What's the real estate temperature: Is it hot or cold? You can always expect to pay less in a cold market, more in a hot market.

The property. Is it just a run-of-the-mill investment, or does it have phenomenal potential? If it's common, offer less, far less. These properties are a dime a dozen. If it's exceptional, you'll want to offer more. Keep in mind that the more run down the property, the less it's likely to bring. The more spruced up it is (the better it shows), the higher the price.

The asking price. Is the seller already asking the right market value, or is it too high or too low? If the house is already priced below market, you may want to offer closer to full price. If it's priced above market (which most properties usually are), you'll want to offer much less.

Your perspective. Remember, you can make money in real estate simply by paying full price and holding onto the property. If you're satisfied doing this, offer just 5 percent below market. However, if you've decided to be a cutthroat investor, offer far less.

Knowing What the Home's True Market Value Is

Learning this is a good starting point. Begin by going to an agent or checking one of the many Internet Web sites that offer comparative market analyses (CMAs) such as www.zillow.com or www.reiclub.com to start. A CMA takes a look at all similar properties sold within the previous six months to a year within the area. You then compare the sold properties and prices with the subject property and its asking price. Add for extra features the subject has. Subtract for features the sold properties had that the subject home lacks. By comparison, you can quickly determine the market value of the property.

Keep in mind, however, that a CMA tells you only what similar properties sold for a few months to about a year ago. It usually doesn't tell you what they're selling for right now. In a rising market, you have to add a certain percentage for recent appreciation. In a falling market, you need to subtract for recent and future price depreciation.

Deciding How Much to Lowball

Your Lowball Offer. Now decide on how much to lowball. You may want to offer as much as 25 percent, or more, less than the asking price. However, that's usually considered just a test offer to see what the water's like. In all but a very cold market, a seller's likely to simply reject it out of hand. Indeed, the seller may simply ignore the offer and not counter it. That defeats your purpose. The goal of the initial lowball is to get a counteroffer from the seller. Try to offer enough to entice the seller to at least respond.

The Seller's Counteroffer. The counteroffer can be very revealing. If it's just $1,000 or so off the asking price (or right at the asking price), you can assume that this seller won't budge much. Then it's time to fish or cut bait. Either move up closer to the seller's price or move on.

TIP You'll probably need to make lots of lowball offers playing the odds until you chance upon a seller who, for one reason or another, is willing to drop the price.

On the other hand, when the seller's counter drops the price significantly, you know you've got a fish hooked on the line. Now it's a matter of negotiating the lowest possible price.

Your Counteroffer in Response to the Seller's Counteroffer. After a seller counters at a significantly lower price (but not as low as you've originally offered), you've really got only three alternatives:

1. *Accept* the seller's counter as is if you think it's low enough.
2. *Counter* at a price lower than the seller offered, typically halfway between your original offer and the seller's first counteroffer.
3. *Repeat* your original offer if you think it's a good price.

Compromising at halfway between the seller's last offer and your original offer (number 2 above) may land the deal. Or the seller may cut the remaining distance in half again with yet another counter. Either way, you're well along toward getting the home at a reasonable price.

Sticking to your original offer (reoffering it as your first counter) has some negotiating drawbacks. It tells the seller to take it or leave it. It says you're not willing to compromise.

A certain percentage of the time (no one knows how much because each deal is unique, but it's not high), you'll win by holding pat. The seller will indeed capitulate and accept your original offer. This usually happens, however, only in a cold market and with a desperate seller.

More likely the seller will simply throw up his or her hands and say there's no dealing with you. The seller will then simply walk away. After all, if you don't raise your offer, what choice have you left the seller but to take your offer or quit?

My suggestion is that unless you think your original lowball offer is actually realistic, always counter the seller's counter, even if you come up only $1,000 or so. It keeps the negotiations open. And it gives the seller another chance to come down even more.

Eventually, you'll get the house you want at the price you want to pay. Or you'll move on.

And don't fall in love with the property. Always remember that you're not going to live in the property, a tenant is. Furthermore, you're eventually going to resell. Therefore, buy with an eye to what a tenant will accept (making it easiest for you to maintain) and a new owner will like.

That may not be such good advice when seeking financing, as we'll see in Chapter 10. However, it's excellent advice when making offers on property. When buying an investment, the last thing you want is an emotional attachment.

TRAP

Business is business and personal is personal, and the two should never mix.

Maintaining Your Objectivity

While all this might sound obvious, it's sometimes difficult to execute. For example, you're looking at a lovely little single-family cottage with an adorable white picket fence in front, French windows all around, lush white carpeting inside, and tile countertops in the kitchen and bath. To you it looks like a wonderful place to live. So when the owner wants a few thousand more than the market will bear for the place, you're willing to pop for it. After all, it's something you simply must have.

Mistake.

Bad mistake.

If you were going to live there, you might keep repainting that fence white, never break one of the French window panels, take your shoes off before walking on the carpeting, and scrub the grout between tiles. But you cannot expect a tenant to do the same things. Remember, unless it's a flipper, you're planning to rent it out for a while, at least until prices go up and you sell. That means you're looking for *low* maintenance. All of the items just mentioned are high maintenance.

What you want is a property that doesn't require constant repainting, that when a window breaks, it's easy and relatively inexpensive to replace, with carpeting (probably beige or brown) that doesn't show dirt, and with laminate or other solid-surface countertops that won't get stained (and require expensive repair and regrouting).

All of which is to say, look at each property with an investor's eye, not a home buyer's eye. It's not for you to live in; therefore, it

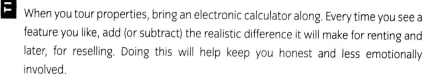

When you tour properties, bring an electronic calculator along. Every time you see a feature you like, add (or subtract) the realistic difference it will make for renting and later, for reselling. Doing this will help keep you honest and less emotionally involved.

doesn't have to meet your personal standards. All it has to do is make good business sense.

Deciding How Much of Your Own Money to Put into the Purchase

For most people, this is not a difficult decision. Most real estate investors have very little cash; consequently, they are always looking for low-down-payment properties—the lower, the better. (We'll discuss low down payments further in Chapter 10.) However, some of those new to investing worry that a low down payment accompanying a lowball offer will scare a seller into declining. Put up a big down payment, they reason, and the seller will be more inclined to accept a lower offer.

Not true; not even close to true.

Unless there's creative financing involved such that the seller is putting up the money for you to purchase the home, the deal is always all cash to the seller. It doesn't matter whether you put 30 percent down or 5 percent down—the seller gets cashed out! (The only party it makes a difference to is the lender, who will determine the minimum down payment for you.)

As a consequence, as long as you can come up with a letter from a lender showing that you are approved for the required financing, the seller won't care a whit how big a down payment you're offering.

Therefore, it's usually to your advantage to put as little down as possible.

Many new investors will argue against putting a minimal down payment into an investment property, worrying about the higher monthly payments this will cause. They realize that the less of your cash you put into the property, the higher your monthly payments will be. Contrarily, the more cash you put in, the lower will be your monthly payments. One way to avoid creating an alligator, they reason, is to put enough money into the property to get the monthly payments (expenses) down to the point where rental income will cover them. That way you can keep the property over a long period of time and not have to worry about negative cash flow.

Again, that's often a mistake.

The rule is this: don't put *more* money into an investment house to get a lower payment. Instead, find a different, less expensive, better-financed investment house.

Keeping Your Personal Financing Separate from Your Business Financing

If it's your own home, it may indeed make good sense to put more cash down. Most people like the security a low monthly house payment affords. But it doesn't make sense for an investment property. Rather, look for a home with higher rental income.

Remember, if you put 5 percent down and the property appreciates 5 percent, you've made 100 percent profit. But if you put 20 percent down and the property goes up 5 percent, you've only made 25 percent profit.

At 20 percent down, it will take you four times longer to make the same profit as it would with 5 percent down.

Further, keep in mind that the more money you stick into a property, the less you have available to invest elsewhere. If you have $40,000 and put 20 percent down on a $200,000 home, you've use up all of your cash (ignoring closing costs for the moment).

On the other hand, if you only put 10 percent down ($20,000), you still have half your cash left to buy yet another home. (If you can get away with only 5 percent cash down, you could theoretically buy four homes.) The more homes, the more profit.

Holding Back Some Cash in Reserve

Providing you find the right property, putting the smallest amount down works best with investment property. That doesn't mean, however, that you invest all of your cash in real estate. Common sense dictates that you always keep a reserve in case of emergencies. I, personally, tend to be conservative and keep a reserve of about 25 percent of my assets in cash. That's enough to keep my finances solvent, and it allows me to handle almost anything the market throws at me.

Other investors who are more daring keep only about 10 or even 5 percent of their working capital in reserve. They are less prepared for a long vacancy period, a big repair bill, or even a downturn in the market. On the other hand, they make bigger profits as long as things go well.

TIP

Try to avoid being "land poor." That means that while you own a lot of property, you don't have any cash on hand for business or personal needs and emergencies.

I believe that the amount of cash reserve that you keep must be determined by your sleep index. If it keeps you up worrying at night, your reserves are too low. Increase them until you can sleep comfortably. That's the right amount.

By the way, your reserves don't need to be in the form of actual cash. They can be in any form that can be quickly converted to cash. That includes the following:

Savings accounts
Bonds

Stocks

Lines of credit

A *line of credit* allows a borrower to draw cash out as needed and pay it back as desired. It is easy to place on properties on which you have large equities. If it's a home you occupy, the line of credit is called a *home equity loan*.

The Bottom Line

Work at making lowball offers. Yes, you'll lose out on some, perhaps most, of the offers you make. But chances are that the ones you do get might be terrific deals.

Sweet Deals in Foreclosures

A lender's bad loan is an investor's gold mine.

Whenever we come off a "boom" (or "bubble") in the real estate cycle, the number of residential foreclosures increases dramatically. There are always buyers who get in over their heads with payments that are higher than they can handle.

This was particularly the case with the last boom cycle when bizarre financing was available such as *option mortgages* that allowed the borrower to determine how big a payment he or she would make. Of course, smaller payments meant that some of the interest due, rather than being paid as part of the monthly payments, was instead added to the mortgage, which grew in size. And typically after three years these option mortgages would *reset*, meaning that the borrower then had to make full payments, which were sometimes double the amount they had been paying each month.

The borrower had three choices: refinance, resell, or lose the property to foreclosure. Often interest rates had risen and the borrower no longer had the resources to refinance, the market was too soft to resell, and hence, the property was lost to foreclosure. That's where you, the investor, come in.

As an investor, you may be able to buy a property in foreclosure for a bargain price. Then you can either hold it for the long run or in some cases flip it. For the adventurous investor, foreclosures can be sweet deals.

But they also can be tricky. You must know what you're doing. And the first thing to understand is that there are three stages of foreclosure:

Stage 1. The seller can't make payments and the lender puts the mortgage in default. The title to the property at this time still rests with the owner. You must buy it from him or her. This is sometimes referred to as "preforeclosure."

Stage 2. After a legally determined period of time the lender "sells" the property to the highest bidder "on the courthouse steps." You can bid at these public auctions, although there are all sorts of traps.

Stage 3. If the lender at the auction was the highest bidder, it then takes the title to property. However, lenders don't want to be owners. So as quickly as possible, they attempt to resell. These lender-owned properties are called real estate owned properties (REOs) when they are private properties and repossessions (repos) when they are government-owned properties.

At each stage the opportunities and challenges are different. We'll consider each separately.

Buying Directly from a Seller in Preforeclosure

What we're concerned with here is stage 1. The seller can't or won't make payments. He or she is motivated to sell the property hoping to recoup any equity and save a credit rating. This seller is going to listen to any offer that you make.

In a strong market, one would think that there aren't any sellers in foreclosure. But that's not the case. The foreclosure rate in good times may be a fraction of what it is in bad times. But in any times there are still plenty of foreclosures. Sellers are always losing property. Some of the more common reasons include these:

- The seller has overborrowed and can't make the payments.
- There is an illness, death, or divorce in the family, and no one takes charge of maintaining the property, allowing it to fall through the cracks into foreclosure.
- The seller moved and listed the house. But the agent was terrible and didn't find any buyers, and now the seller, at a distance, just won't or can't deal with the house anymore.
- The seller simply doesn't care about the property (rare, but it does happen).

How to Find Foreclosures

Online Services. Today, most of the properties in foreclosure are listed online. There are dozens if not hundreds of these online listing companies. Many will give the street address and, in some cases, some helpful information about the sellers and borrowers.

Of course, most charge a fee for the service. However, even if there is a fee, it can be worthwhile to get the information. Just be sure you look for foreclosures in your area. These services tend to be national in scope. Check out www.foreclosures.com.

For-Sale-by-Owner Sellers. A good place to find properties in foreclosure is to look for "For Sale by Owner" (FSBO) signs. Sometimes this person will have decided to forego the traditional listing process and instead wants to dispose of the property on his or her own. (The seller may have had it listed, but the listing expired with no results.) Now facing foreclosure, the seller is at the last desperate stage.

Typically such FSBO efforts are nonproductive and are being pursued only halfheartedly as the house moves closer to foreclosure. In fact, the only effort may be a sign in the front yard that says "For Sale by Owner." (Also check out www.owners.com.)

TIP Look for foreclosures close to home. You want a rental that's less than 45 minutes away from where you live so you won't have trouble servicing it.

Once you've determined *where* you want to buy your investment house, begin touring the area. Drive up and down the streets. Chances are you'll run into an occasional FSBO. Stop, introduce yourself, and talk to the seller. It will most often be the case that the seller is trying to sell the property as a FSBO just to save paying a commission. When he or she can't sell it as a FSBO (which will happen more than half the time), the seller will list it with an agent. There's no foreclosure possibility here.

However, occasionally you will find someone who actually is in foreclosure. When you do, you've got your motivated seller.

Agents. Another way to find foreclosures is to ask the local real estate agents. Agents will know if any of their sellers are in foreclosure.

Of course, there is the chance that the agents will attempt to buy such properties themselves or "give" them to relatives or friends. That, of course, is why you need to know many agents. You can be that lucky person.

Title insurance and trust companies also know about foreclosures. This is particularly the case in states that use the *trust deed* device instead of the older *mortgage* device. (Currently over 40 states use the trust deed as the preferred lending device.)

To understand why, it's important to know that in a traditional mortgage, there are two parties—the borrower and the lender. To foreclose, the lender must begin legal proceedings in court.

With a trust deed, in contrast, there are three parties: the borrower (*trustor*), the lender (*beneficiary*), and the *trustee*. When the lender loans money to the borrower, the borrower gives to that third party, the trustee, the right to sell that house if he or she doesn't keep up the payments on that loan. The trustee, in short, holds the foreclosure power.

When the borrower doesn't pay, the lender notifies the trustee that the borrower is in default, and the trustee begins foreclosure proceedings.

Now here's the important part with regard to finding properties in trust deed foreclosure: The trustee named in the trust deed is usually a title insurance and trust company. These companies are set up to handle the position of trustee and to handle foreclosures, which is why they are so named by most lenders.

Hence, if you become known to a title insurance and trust company, they'll be willing to let you have a list of properties they have put into foreclosure. They do not widely advertise or disseminate such lists but instead make them available to their clients and "friends." (A good number of investors have gotten rich in the past simply by becoming fast friends with a title insurance company officer.)

Of course, there's nothing secret about such a list. It's just most convenient to get it from a title insurance company. If you can't, however, there is another alternative.

Newspapers. The first step in foreclosure is the filing of a *notice of default*. This notice usually must be filed with the county recorder's office. (This applies to mortgages as well as trust deeds.) To obtain this information, you could spend some time at the county recorder's office checking for notices of default that have been filed. Few of us, however, have such time to spend.

An alternative may be to check the "legal newspaper" in your area. Most well-populated areas have a newspaper whose sole purpose is to carry legal notices. If you've only subscribed to the larger consumer newspapers, you may have never heard of it. But a call to any title insurance company officer or the county clerk's office will confirm its existence and probably get you a number to call.

These specialized newspapers publish legal notices such as doing-business-as (dba) notifications and other types of notifications that people are legally required to publish. In addition, they publish such items as notices of default.

Of course, one of the problems with checking these notices (as well as the notices filed with the county clerk) is that they tend to give the legal description of the property. Instead of saying "256 Orange Street," they may give a tract, block, and map number. Unless you're able to read recorded maps, such information isn't all that helpful. (Often online sites offer the same information, see page 69.)

Private Listing Companies. Which brings us to yet another source: Usually advertised in legal newspapers, *private listing companies,* for a fee, will sell you a list of properties in foreclosure giving their common street address and sometimes the name and phone number of the owner. Be aware, however, that this list is frequently costly, often more than $100 a month. (This is why it's nice to have a friend at a title insurance company who can get you such a list for free!) Just call up and subscribe as you would to any other service.

How to Deal with an Owner in Preforeclosure

Once you find someone who is in foreclosure, it's then up to you to contact the person directly and find out if there is a good deal available for you. With the person's name and phone number in hand, you can give him or her a call. Explain that you're an investor and that you're looking for property in the area. You heard that the person was having some difficulty in making payments, and you're wondering if there's a way to make a win-win situation out of it—the owner gets his or her credit saved (plus, perhaps, some money depending on the owner's equity) and you get the property.

TIP

At the least you should have an address. A reverse phone book may give you a name and number. But if all you have is an address, you can always stop by and knock on the door.

Be forewarned. Some people won't want to talk with you. They may be nasty, even offensive. People in the midst of a foreclosure usually take it personally and may blame everyone but themselves for it. Forget them. They can't be helped, and most likely they will lose their house and their credit.

Others will be happy, even eager to talk. Those are the ones you want to work with. When you find such an owner, you have to determine what it's going to cost you to take over the property.

The Costs of Righting a Foreclosure

What you can offer to the owner is to make up the back payments and penalties and save the owner's credit rating in exchange for the title to the property. In other words, you can offer to *right the fore-closure*. You might be able to do this in some financing situations and consequently get a property for virtually no money down plus whatever equity the owner may have. In other situations, the loan may not be *assumable*. If that's the case, you may not only have to make up back payments and penalties but also secure a new loan with accompanying points and fees.

In short, it may cost you many thousands of dollars to take over a particular property and bail out the owner. You may find that by the time you add up the costs, it simply isn't worthwhile.

Potential Costs Involved in Righting a Foreclosure

- **Back payments.** These could be as much as six months of payments or more.
- **Penalties.** Each month that the payment is late usually incurs a penalty. In addition, there may be additional penalties as time periods in the foreclosure process expire.
- **New loan costs.** These can include points, fees, title insurance, and other costs. Typically these costs will amount to about 5 percent of the loan amount; on a $100,000 mortgage, figure about $5,000.
- **Fixing up the property.** The former owner may not have kept the place in great shape once he or she learned that he or she was going to lose it. You could have to spend several thousand in refurbishing and relandscaping.

It's important that you calculate these costs as accurately as possible before you make any kind of offer to the owner. You may find that it simply isn't worth your time to attempt to right the foreclosure and take over the property. Here's an example of how this might happen.

Case History: Cynthia's Investment House

Jamie bought his southern California home in 2005, right at the height of the last boom in prices. He paid $650,000 for it. He put 15 percent down and took out an interest-only mortgage. The mortgage had an option that allowed him to defer payments, which were then added to the principal of the loan.

In 2007 the mortgage reset. Suddenly it became a fully amortized adjustable-rate mortgage (ARM). This meant that he had to make principal and interest payments, which turned out to be almost twice as much as he had been paying before. Suddenly he couldn't handle the payments.

Even worse, he had lost his old job and had taken a new one at a lower salary. Now he couldn't afford to refinance. And the soft market made it impossible to sell. Jamie got behind in his payments and the lender foreclosed.

The mortgage on his house was now nearly $590,000. He listed the property for $700,000, enough to cover the listing commission, closing costs, back payments and penalties, and something for himself. But by the time he listed, the market had turned soft. The property was so overpriced that there were no offers and no lookers. Eventually the listing expired, and now Jamie was trying to sell it as a FSBO.

Cynthia was an investor with good credit who had lined up lenders and who was looking for foreclosures. Jamie's name had popped up on a list of properties in foreclosure on a Web site, and she gave him a call. He seemed pleased to talk about his problems, so she went to see him.

The property was in a good tenant market, and Jamie was certainly a motivated seller. So Cynthia was excited about the prospects and began to figure out the costs involved:

Costs Involved in Correcting the Foreclosure	
Three months' back payments:	$10,500
Penalties:	$400
Fixing up house:	$3,100
Securing new loan:	+$12,000 (Jamie's old loan was not assumable.)
Total costs:	$24,000

It would cost Cynthia roughly $24,000 to pay off Jamie's existing loan (including back payments and penalties) and other costs. The bottom line was that if she did this, she'd have an instant equity of roughly $40,000 in the home, given then current values. For her it was a no-brainer. So she paid to have a title search to see who really owned the property. It turned out it was still in both

Jamie's and his wife's names, so she would need two signatures on a purchase agreement. Also, she learned there were no other loans or liens on the home.

TIP

One of the big problems in buying from an owner in foreclosure is knowing what you're getting. Sometimes the seller won't disclose additional loans or liens on the property. When buying a foreclosure from a seller, it is up to the investor to check the condition of the title. Buying title insurance as additional protection is always a good idea.

However, there was the matter of convincing Jamie. From Jamie's perspective, he had roughly $100,000 in equity. He wanted someone to pay him this full amount to take over his house.

Cynthia thought about it, and then made Jamie the following offer.

Cynthia's Offer. If Jamie would sign the house over to Cynthia, she would pay off the old loan and all the back payments, penalties, and interest. (She would do this by securing a new loan with her good credit, but that was none of Jamie's business.) Jamie would walk away free and clear, his credit intact.

Jamie blew up at this offer. He accused Cynthia of trying to steal his home. Where, he wanted to know, was his equity?

Cynthia responded that Jamie's equity was not the issue; it was his good name. His equity was lost because with his bad credit, caused by his job loss, he could not refinance. Also, he could not sell; he had tried that route without success. Further, within weeks the foreclosure process would be completed, and Jamie would not only lose his home but his good name as well. That could adversely affect his ability to obtain credit for years to come. Cynthia could make all of this go away.

Jamie said he'd think about it. He did. He called Cynthia a week later, with foreclosure staring him in the face only days away, and he said he'd make the deal *if* she'd give him $7,500 for his equity.

Cynthia agreed, providing that she could get financing in time to stave off the foreclosure. Cynthia had it all put in writing in the form of a purchase agreement drawn up by an attorney, and she had Jamie and his wife both sign (which took an extra day to accomplish).

TIP

When dealing with people in foreclosure, leave nothing to the spoken word. If it isn't in writing properly worded and signed, it isn't. Further, when dealing with anyone involved in a divorce, make sure that both parties sign.

Cynthia then immediately went to the existing lender who agreed to extend the foreclosure procedure for two weeks for a partial payment of the amount owed. She then proceeded to secure electronic quick funding of a new mortgage, took the title to the property, and paid off the old loan and foreclosure costs. Then the only problem was getting Jamie to leave. She had to give him an extra $500 to move out!

Nevertheless, she had quickly purchased an investment house with nearly $40,000 in equity.

TIP

While the above example illustrates a win-win situation, it isn't always that way. Sometimes a buyer will take unfair advantage of a seller going through a foreclosure, and the buyer will purchase the home for significantly less than the seller paid for it. (Cynthia bought the house for roughly the same price that Jamie paid.) Some states have enacted laws to protect owners in foreclosure from unscrupulous buyers. Such laws allow a certain period of time for *recision* of a sales agreement when the seller is in default on a mortgage. The period of time can vary from a few days to as long as six months or more after the sale. Before you buy a house that is in foreclosure, be sure to find out about and comply with these protective laws so that later on, the original seller does not come back and demand that you return the home. To avoid these types of problems in buying a home from a seller who is in foreclosure, check with a good real estate attorney in your state who can alert you to the laws and regulations that bear on the particular foreclosure situation you are working with.

The obvious advantage of dealing with an owner in foreclosure is that you can get a property at the right price for the current market. If the house happens to be run down and in need of repair, you may get a price far below market. In short, dealing with owners who are in foreclosure is a way to find bargain properties. On the other hand, it's usually a big hassle, there are many unknowns (such as additional loans and/or liens on the property), and working with a lender can be problematical.

Buying from a Lender at a Foreclosure Auction

Another way of purchasing a property in foreclosure is by actually buying it when it is sold "on the courthouse steps."

At the time of the foreclosure auction (or sale), the lender always offers the full price of the mortgage (or trust deed). But there is nothing to prevent you or anyone else from offering more.

Your offer, however, must be in the form of cash, so you will have to work out the financing in advance. And you will receive no title insurance or other guarantees as to the status of the property. (You might, for example, think you're bidding on a first mortgage only to find that it's a second or third. This could be catastrophic for you.) You'll want to secure title insurance as soon as possible.

It is beyond the scope of this book to go into detail on buying homes at foreclosure auctions as this is a topic for a separate tome. Suffice to say that it is usually the venue of attorneys and those well-versed in real estate practice and law. It can also be a highly profitable area. If you are interested in it, you might consider consulting with a real estate agent and attorney in your area who specialize in the field.

Buying from a Lender in the REO Market

REO stands for "real estate owned." It's what happens to the property after the lender buys it at auction in a foreclosure sale.

There's money to be made in these lender-owned properties. Sometimes they can be purchased for below-market value, particularly if they are in distressed condition. Other times, though, you might pay market value, or the lender may offer special financing at a lower-than-market interest rate or with other appealing terms and bonuses.

A friend of mine recently bought three REOs near Phoenix, Arizona. All three had been owned by the same lender who made him a deal on the lot: two at market and one substantially below. My friend then flipped the below-market property and fixed up the other two and rented them out. He intends to sell those within a year or two for a substantial profit. And he did it all with the lender's financing and almost no money of his own.

Can you do the same thing?

It's possible, depending on how determined you are. REOs are a special part of the real estate market, one that is sometimes covered in a blanket of secrecy.

How Foreclosures Become REO Properties

From a foreclosure perspective, there's an obvious difference between a lender and an investor, although most of us never give it a second thought. An investor, like you, is a person who buys property and hopes to eventually resell it for a profit. A lender, such as a bank, loans out money hoping to receive interest in return. Most investors don't want to be lenders. And lenders, I can assure you, do not want to be investors.

Indeed, the only time banks and other lending institutions become investors is when their mortgages and other loans go bad.

Then they are forced to foreclose and take the collateral, real estate in this case, back—REOs.

If you're a financial officer in a lending institution, R-E-O are three letters you never want to hear. The reason is that while a performing mortgage (one where the borrower makes payments) is considered an asset, a REO is considered a liability. It moves from the asset side of the accounting books to the liability side and can adversely affect the lender's financial stability. Additionally, regulators may require the lender to put up additional capital to insure against loss should the lender not be able to sell the REO for the amount it has in it. Too many REOs and the lender will go bankrupt.

Why Lenders Make Bad Loans. Although with the help of computerized profiling lenders are getting a lot better at making good loans, they still make a fairly large number of bad ones.

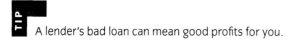

TIP A lender's bad loan can mean good profits for you.

To understand why lenders make bad loans, you must consider the plight of the lending officer. The most important officer in a lending institution is the one who makes loans, good loans. (A *good loan* is one that the borrower repays on time.) A lending officer who makes good loans can be highly rewarded.

The problem is that usually there is far more money to lend out than there are qualified borrowers for it. As a result, lending officers are caught between a rock and a hard place. If they produce the volume their employer wants, they are bound to get some bad loans. If they go only for good loans, they can't keep up the volume.

Consequently, almost all lending institutions make some marginal loans and as a result, have some problems. (And the turnover rate for lending officers tends to be high!)

What Happens to Bad Mortgages? Once a mortgage is nonperforming for a period of time and the borrower appears unable to correct the deficiencies (back interest payments and penalties), the lender will begin foreclosure.

TIP

Contrary to popular belief, most lenders do not start foreclosure when the first payment is late. Typically they will wait three to six months before beginning foreclosure proceedings, hoping the borrower will right the loan. (Government regulators also insist that they make every effort to help the borrower get back on track.) Remember, lenders don't want the property back—they want a performing loan.

The loan is considered nonperforming throughout the foreclosure process. However, once the foreclosure is complete and the lender takes the title to the property, the mortgage stops being nonperforming. It, in fact, stops being a mortgage at all. It is erased from the mortgage category and, as noted above, is instead placed on the books as a property valued at the amount of the mortgage. However, since the property generates no interest (lenders don't usually rent out their REOs), it becomes a liability.

As noted earlier, it doesn't take long for a lender to get into capital reserve troubles if it has too many REOs. Ten mortgages at $600,000 each converted to REOs ties up $6 million of capital. It is to the lender's advantage, therefore, to get rid of that property as soon as possible. It wants to sell it and thus convert the REO back into either cash, which can be loaned out, or a new mortgage, which amounts to the same thing.

The point is that lenders want to get rid of REOs in the worst way. They will go a long way to get rid of any that they have, including making you a sweetheart deal on them. Thus, some of the best deals in a down market can be obtained by buying lender REOs.

REO Properties: The Secret Investments

There is one stumbling block, however, to buying REOs from lenders. Almost universally, lenders won't admit publicly that they have an REO problem. Many won't admit they even have any REOs. Thus, you can't usually just walk in and ask to buy one.

This certainly seems to work against a lender's best interests, at least on the surface. One would think that they would be out there advertising those properties as heavily as possible. Yet, they don't. Do you ever recall seeing a lender advertising under its own name for REO buyers? It normally just doesn't happen. (Most people aren't even familiar with the term "REO.")

The reasoning of the lenders is threefold:

First, a lender doesn't want to alert federal watchdogs that it has an REO problem. Keeping up a good face can mean the difference between remaining in business or being considered insolvent.

Second, depositors are wary about where they place their money. Yes, we know every account is guaranteed to $100,000. But how many of us want to put that guarantee to the test? We might bolt if we thought the lender were shaky.

Third, there are holders of amounts larger than $100,000 who frequently move funds from lender to lender trying to tie up the highest interest rates. These large depositors are not insured and will pull their funds at the slightest whiff of trouble from a lending institution. Hence, lenders are very careful not to admit they have many REOs, if for no other reason than to protect their own image.

Finally, there is the matter of the real estate market. If it became widely known that lenders had an overhang of homes ready to dump on the market in a particular area, it could adversely affect prices. This would backfire for the lenders because it would result in their receiving less money for the properties they are trying to sell.

Therefore, the lenders are close-mouthed about their REOs for one of the following reasons:

1. They don't want to alert federal watchdogs.
2. They don't want to scare away depositors.
3. They don't want to hurt the real estate market.

How to Find REO Properties

All of the above reasons present a problem to you, as an investor, who wants to get an especially good deal on an REO. How do you find out about REOs when the lenders keep mum about them?

The truth is that while lenders keep quiet about REOs as far as the general public is concerned, they can be open about them to buyers. After all, they do want to sell them in order to get the money invested back at work as a mortgage.

Most lenders list their REOs with a local real estate agent who then puts them on the market at full price. You can buy REOs in your area simply by checking with local agents. They are also listed on Web sites such as www.foreclosure.com. (See below.)

On the other hand, you want to buy these REOs at discount, not at full market price. Full market price does you little good. One way is to convince the lender to let you bid on its REOs *before* it lists them. Basically you need to let a lender know that you are a sophisticated investor. You need to let the lender know that you understand what a REO is and that you'd like to bid on one in the raw, so to speak.

Once the lender understands that you're special and not part of the public interested only in deposits, the lender may open up, at least in a limited way.

An Example. I recently called up the main offices of a large lender in the San Jose, California, area. I asked to talk to the officer in charge of the REO department. For a few minutes the operator seemed confused. The company had a loan department, an escrow department, and an operations officer. She didn't have a REO department listed.

I asked to talk to the operations officer, and my call was put through to her. (The operations officer handles day-to-day operations of the lending institution.) I explained to her that I was an investor and wanted to speak to someone in the REO department. I was given a number to call.

When I called the number, I explained that I was an investor interested in purchasing an REO direct, before the lender fixed it up and listed it. Could I get a list of REOs available from the lending institution?

No, I was told. No such list existed. (Hah! The lender didn't have a list of its own REOs? Come on, now!)

I understood that I was just a voice on the other end of the line. I was someone unknown to the REO officer who wasn't about to release information considered delicate. So I tried a different ploy.

I said I was looking for REOs in a particular area. I gave the community, a rather small district of the city. Did the lender have any REOs in that area?

There was a pause, and then the officer said yes, there were three. If I was interested in them, I could come down and fill out an identity form, and they would then give me the addresses so I could go out and look them over.

Success!

As I said, it really isn't hard. But you have to do it for each lender, and it's a little bit different each time.

Real Estate Agents. Frequently when you call a lender, as noted, you will be told that all REOs are listed with local real estate agents. The agents handle the sale for the lender who has no direct sales to the public.

Okay. If you must, deal with the agent. You can try to work a lowball deal with the agent.

I have bought REOs through agents, and it can work out okay. If the lender wants to pay a commission to a broker for handling the sale, it's no skin off my nose.

Typically a lender will designate a particular broker to handle all its REOs in an area. Usually it is one of the larger and more active offices.

After you find out who the agent is from the lender, just call up the office and ask to speak to "Jill Smith" who handles the REOs for XYZ lender. Usually there is one agent who does this, although in large offices sometimes all the agents "cobroke" or work on REO sales.

Talk to the agent. Explain you're an investor looking for a good REO deal. Get to know the agent a bit, and allow him or her to get to know you.

I recall one REO I bought a few years ago in this manner from an agent. When told there were none available, I asked if any had recently been sold. Yes, I was told. One had, but it was in escrow.

Fine, I said. Could I see it?

Certainly. I was given the address and the agent later took me to the property. It was a nice house—run down but in a good area and at a good price. I said I would like to make a "back-up" offer on it. If the current offer fell through, I'd like mine to be considered.

Fine, said the agent, and he wrote it up. My reasoning was that most active investors, those who own lots of property, are spread thin. As a result, they often have little cash to put down or their income isn't sufficient to cover new financing. In addition, over the years they may have lost one or two properties, and the foreclosures show up on their credit reports. They may even be land poor because although they own several valuable properties, they are unable to get their cash out. These active investors frequently know about REOs and often make offers that are accepted. But also frequently, these people don't qualify for financing, and the deals fall through.

This happened to be the case with me. The first buyer was rejected for a mortgage by the lender. My back-up offer, already written up, was submitted. And subsequently, I got the property.

No, it won't happen that way every time. But it will happen that way often enough to make it worthwhile trying.

Fixing Up a REO Property

REOs are often in distressed condition. Consider the situation from this point of view: If you were the borrower and were losing the house, your equity, and your credit rating, would you be anxious to keep watering the lawn or to clean up when you left?

Most borrowers who lose their property through foreclosure not only do not clean up but they often actually go out of their way to mess up the property. Their reaction, naturally enough, is anger, and since they really can't take it out on anyone personally, they typically take it out on the property.

I have seen REOs where the sinks and toilets were ripped out, where all the windows were broken, where fecal material was rubbed into the carpets, where holes were smashed into the walls, and on and on. (I've often speculated that had the former owners spent half as much energy trying to make the payments as they did messing up the house, they might still own the property.)

When you get to the REO, it may still be in the terrible shape in which the lender got it back. Or it may be fixed up.

Lenders are no fools (although their lending policies sometimes suggest otherwise). They know that a distressed property will get them a distressed price. On the other hand, if they fix it up even just cosmetically, they stand to get a far better price.

But if you arrive on the spot just as the REO is acquired and offer to take it "as is," the lender may agree. After all, the time spent fixing up the property is, once again, lost interest to the lender.

Thus, when you find an REO in distressed condition, don't turn your head away in disgust. You're not looking at a disaster; you may be looking at an opportunity.

Calculating Fix-Up and Clean-Up Costs. Experienced investors can estimate clean-up and fix-up costs in just a few minutes. But that's a result of their experience.

If you're new to the game, it's going to take you longer. If you find a distressed REO that otherwise fits your needs in terms of location, tenant market, and so on (see the next section), calculate the costs to fix it up.

You may have to call a painter, plumber, and electrician. (In truth, to be successful, you're going to have to eventually make contact with subcontractors who can do this for you, or you're going to have to learn how to do it yourself.) You may have to calculate the costs of having someone come in and clean out the mess. You'll have to calculate relandscaping costs and so forth. The following list contains some of the items you need to consider.

What to Consider When Refurbishing a Distressed Property

Clean-up. This may include washing the kitchen appliances such as the stove and also all of the sinks and baths.

Carpeting and pads. These may need to be cleaned or replaced. Watch out for pet urine in the carpet; often the smell cannot be removed and the carpet must be replaced.

Plumbing. This may include replacing fixtures such as the baths, sinks, and toilets.

Electrical. This might mean replacing or putting in new light fixtures and repairing any damage to outlets and switches.

Painting. This may need to be done inside and outside.

Landscaping. This could include installing a new front lawn and garden, but you can often get by without fixing up the backyard too elaborately by just cutting down the weeds.

Fencing. Often this is broken down and needs repair.

Roof. Check for leaks that have to be fixed.

Plaster or wallboard. Check for needed repairs such as holes that need to be filled in.

Doors and door handles. Replace or repair these as needed.

Windows and screens. Replace these as needed.

Locks. Replace these as a security measure.

Any other broken or damaged item.

As you can see, the list is fairly long. It can also be fairly costly. It's important that you get as accurate a cost figure as possible. Remember, you'll be paying for it. Also, don't forget to include a figure for your time and effort, especially if you're going to be doing the work yourself.

TRAP

REOs are often in distressed neighborhoods. Remember to judge the neighborhood first and foremost. Don't become enraptured with dreams of refurbishing the house until you're convinced that the neighborhood warrants it. If there's a high crime and vandalism rate in the neighborhood, you may find that as quickly as you clean up and fix up, there's someone coming around to tear down and mess up. That's a hopeless situation, one of the worst, and you want to avoid it.

Making an Offer for a REO Property

Once you've done your homework in determining that the REO is a good prospect in terms of location, rental market, and so on, as outlined earlier, and you've determined the costs to bring it into rentable shape (unless you plan to flip it), you need to determine what you're going to offer the lender.

Keep in mind that everything in real estate, especially pertaining to REOs, is negotiable. The lender may have set a price, but you don't have to pay it. You can make a lower offer, or you can ask for favorable terms.

TRAP

Good REO property is in high demand by investors. Keep in mind that there may be many offers on the house you are considering. The lender, naturally enough, is going to accept the best.

As a consequence, you need to make your offer as sweet as possible, without hurting. I can recall one REO investor who beat me out on a house a few years back by offering nearly $25,000 more than I offered. The lender, whom I knew fairly well, asked me if I wanted to raise my offer. I reexamined my figures and declined. I couldn't see a profit for me at the higher costs. So the lender gave the property to the other bidder.

As it turned out, the other bidder later admitted that she had overpaid and lost money on the deal. Remember, getting the property is only one battle. Winning the war means ultimately making a profit. If there's no profit, you're just spinning your wheels.

Offering All Cash to the Lender. The simplest offer (for the lender, not you) is to offer all cash. This doesn't mean that you need all cash—you can go out and secure financing on the property. It just means that the lender is going to get all cash.

Typically how you arrive at a price for a cash deal is to calculate what the property is going to be worth when it's fixed up. Then work backward subtracting your realistic costs of fixing it up. (Don't forget to deduct interest payments during the fix-up period as well as your own profit.)

The trouble with an all-cash offer is twofold. From the lender's perspective, it means selling for what might amount to a loss. From your perspective, it means going out and finding a separate, new lender who is willing to loan you money on a distressed property, which is not something always easy to find. There may be an easier way.

Demanding Terms from the Lender. Another way is to offer the lender terms. Offer a higher price for the property. In other words, you offer the current value of the home in its present condition, plus what it's worth when fixed up (but that is usually still less than the market price). However, you then request something like the following:

1. The lender makes you a 90 percent (or 100 percent, if possible) loan on the full purchase price at a favorable interest rate for a term of at least three years to five (based on a 30-year amortization). This allows you time to fix up, rent, and hold until the market turns. It also guarantees the lender that it will be out of the property for good after a set amount of time.

2. The lender gives you a *fix-up allowance* equal to your costs of refurbishing the property, all of which is to come out of the new loan. This simply means that the lender will give you cash back out of the new mortgage (typically made in payments as the work is completed) to fix up the property.

3. The lender pays normal closing costs.

The above terms might appeal to a lender for several reasons. The first is the price. The lender can show that it sold the property at a better price than it might otherwise have commanded and that the lender now has a, presumably, performing mortgage on it—an asset. In other words, selling the property at this price and on these terms will mean that there won't be a loss on the books.

Second, the lender won't have to go in and spend time and money fixing up the property itself, something that many lenders are ill-prepared to do.

Third, you are guaranteeing to fix up the property so that in the event you don't make your payments and the lender has to reforeclose, it will be getting the property back in far better shape.

The above rationale can be appealing to many lenders. Some lenders will take it, unless another investor is waiting in the wings and he or she has a sharper pencil than you and has offered more or asked for a smaller fix-up allowance.

Avoiding the Traps in Purchasing REO Properties

It has been estimated that something approaching two-thirds of all REOs are distressed initially and that some of these are simply hopeless. If you're looking at distressed properties, it's important to determine which have possibilities and which are of the hopeless cast. The last thing you want to do is to relieve a lender of a hopeless problem and make it yours.

The important thing to remember is that the REO is most often sold as is, even if the lender refurbished it. The lender-seller makes no commitment to you of any kind. This can result in some bizarre problems.

No Disclosures. The lender may not give you any disclosures regarding the property. It may not be required to under state or federal law. Further, even if it does give you disclosures, they may be useless since it simply may not know what the problems with the property actually are.

Therefore, it's up to you to diligently inspect the property. The help of a good professional home inspector is invaluable here.

Case History: Cracked Slab. Jason bought an REO with a "cracked slab." In his area of the country, houses were typically built on slabs of concrete reinforced with steel instead of the more traditional peripheral foundation and raised wood floor.

Jason's house seemed all right to look at. However, it was on a slight hill, and one side near the kitchen and dining room sank slightly where the slab was cracked.

Jason evaluated it carefully. He even called in a contractor to examine it. The conclusion was that the ground under the slab at the kitchen had moved outward slightly causing the slab to fall. At the worst it was offset about three inches. The contractor said that to fix it "right," he'd have to rip down half the house and rebuild. Alternatively, he could do a cosmetic fix. He figured he could just pour a new layer over the slab, lift up the walls, and the house would be ready to go.

A simple thing to correct, Jason thought. He made an offer on the REO based on the cosmetic change and was successful. A short time later, the house was his.

However, problems appeared as soon as he started refurbishing. It turned out that when the contractor began cutting out pieces of the old slab in order to blend in the new layer of concrete, he discovered that the reinforcing steel was missing. The original builder some 30 years earlier had failed to put it in!

Without steel, the cracked slab was free to move wherever it wanted. Putting a new layer of concrete on the top wouldn't help at all. The new layer would quickly crack, and perhaps sink, as the concrete continued to shift.

In addition, the local building department showed up to ask why the contractor was working without a permit. (A neighbor had seen the work and complained.) The contractor immediately stopped work and applied for a permit, which was denied! The building department said that, given the lack of reinforcing steel, the only way it would allow work to proceed was to tear out the old cement (and half the house) and put in new cement and new steel.

This story does not have a happy ending. Jason complained to the lender. The lender said, "Sorry." Jason had signed an as-is clause. So Jason resold the property to a builder, who did the refurbishing work correctly. However, Jason lost his original down payment and the money he'd spent refurbishing.

Case History: Bad Tenant. Jill bought an REO with a tenant in it. The tenant was there when she examined the property and claimed that he was paying rent to the lender.

Fine, Jill thought. Having a tenant already in place will save me some time and money. She went ahead with the purchase buying the property as is.

Once the deal went through, she went back and introduced herself as the new owner. She told the tenant that he should now pay the rent to her and she showed him the title papers. He slammed the door in her face, wouldn't let her in, and refused to talk to her.

As it turned out, he had been the tenant of the original owner who had rented out the property instead of living in it personally. When the property went into foreclosure, the tenant remained, not paying rent. He hadn't paid rent for the preceding five months and wasn't about to start now.

Jill tried to reason with him but to no avail. So she secured the services of a real estate attorney who, for several thousand dollars and after a period of nine weeks, finally had the man evicted. During that time, of course, Jill couldn't fix up the property, and she had to make mortgage payments, pay taxes, and insurance.

It would have been far better if Jill had insisted that the lender have the tenant removed. The story, however, does have a happy ending. Jill had sufficient margin in the property that even after her hassle with the tenant, she was able to fix the property and rent it out for positive cash flow.

TRAP

Beware of any REO that has anyone living in it. It could be a former tenant or a former owner. Regardless, never take possession and close the deal until the property is vacant. Make it a condition of your purchase.

These two scenarios let you see that REOs are not all peaches and cream. Problems can and do crop up for the unwary.

On the other hand, I and others have bought REOs successfully, and those purchases have gone without incident, and the properties have been resold at a profit. Most, though not all, of the risk can be reduced by simply being careful.

Buying from Government Agencies

The single biggest owner of residential real estate in the country is the federal government. This is not by choice but mainly because of foreclosures. The government runs a host of programs that aid home buyers with financing. When those home buyers run into trouble and can't make their payments, ultimately it's the government that squares things with lenders and takes the homes back. Then it has the job of reselling them.

I know of several real estate investors who, over the years in good times and bad, have made a healthy living buying and reselling these government repossessions (or repos). Sometimes they are able to quickly flip these properties. Most times they simply buy, fix up, and rent them for a time and then resell them (or refinance or trade them).

The basic procedure for purchasing a government repo is fairly similar throughout various agencies. In most cases, but not all,

TRAP

Be careful of being too enthusiastic about flipping government repos. The federal government has investigated investors who have made unconscionable profits at the expense of the government by buying and quickly flipping repos. The allegations are that the investors, sometimes in collusion with lenders and appraisers, bought the government repos at artificially low costs and then jacked up the prices and quickly resold the properties to unqualified buyers at high prices for low or nothing down. When these rebuyers eventually couldn't make the payments, the government had to again foreclose on the same property. And that made the government very unhappy and determined to quash those responsible.

you must purchase the home through a local real estate agent. (The government pays the agent's commission.) However, it's up to you to ferret out where the homes are and to determine if they are worth investing in.

TRAP

Just because it's a government repo doesn't automatically make it a bargain. The government tries to get as high a price as possible for these homes. Sometimes it asks market price or even above!

In many cases the homes are in poor condition. That means that you must thoroughly investigate the property to determine what it will take to put it back into shape. It's rare that you'll get a government repo in good shape at a good price. There are simply too many other people competing for these properties.

At the present time there are over a dozen different government programs that offer properties for sale. (See the list at the end of this chapter.) We're going to look at several of the biggest programs. Keep in mind that these programs change constantly. Be sure to check with the program managers, agents, or others who administer the sale of the homes to find out what the terms and conditions are at the time you're buying.

HUD

The Housing and Urban Development (HUD) Department takes back homes mainly through its Federal Housing Administration (FHA) program. The FHA insures lenders who make loans. When a borrower defaults, the FHA makes good the loan to the lender and takes the property back. At any given time, it may have tens of thousands of repos for sale across the country. You can check on the Internet to see if there are any HUD homes in your area (www.hud.gov/local/sams.ctznhome.html).

Since the homes come back mainly through the FHA program and since that program has maximum loan amounts that are usually under $300,000 as of this writing (the maximum loan amount differs in different areas of the country), you're not likely to find many upscale properties here. Most are going to be in the moderate to low price range.

Additionally, they may not be in the best of condition. HUD usually does not fix up the properties. That means that they may be in anywhere from average to really bad shape. Don't be surprised at the terrible condition in which you may find a HUD repo. Remember, the former owner lost the property to foreclosure. There was little incentive to keep it up. Additionally, since that time there may have been vandalism.

Making an Offer. As noted, you must make your offer through an agent who represents HUD in your local area. Once you locate a home that you're interested in, contact the referred agent and go see the property. The agent can arrange to have you walk through it. You'll also make your offer directly through the agent.

Pricing. HUD tries to sell its homes at fair market prices. However, sometimes this is difficult to determine because of the run-down condition of the properties. Occasionally, particularly if you are sharp at knowing property values, you can find some real bargains here.

Financing. HUD doesn't make loans directly, but it does work with lenders in a variety of programs. You may be able to get in with virtually nothing down, as long as you're intending to occupy the home. If you're buying as an investment, HUD will usually want at least 10 percent down. In other words, your financing needs here are going to be similar to those with any investment property. HUD often looks with extra favor on buyers who submit offers that are a cash-out to HUD. In other words, you get your own outside financing.

Owner-Occupants. As with many government programs, HUD aims to sell its homes to those who will occupy them. Read that as not to investors. Thus, in the initial offer period those who intend to occupy the HUD homes are given priority in their offers. If you're looking for a house to both live in *and* make an investment in, this can be the perfect choice for you.

Investors. However, if there are no owner-occupants who submit offers during the initial offer period or the home does not sell in that time frame, then investors can make offers that will be considered.

Does this mean that you as an investor have a chance only at the leftovers? Not really. Remember, most of these homes are not in great shape, and most owner-occupants are not eager to buy into them. Further, remember that HUD makes an effort to offer them at market price. For casual owner-occupant buyers who don't really know the market, there may not seem like there are any bargains here.

As a result, often these homes are sold to investors.

Fix-Up Allowances. If the home is in bad shape, HUD may offer a fix-up allowance. This can be either in the form of an additional price reduction, or a special fix-up loan. However, in order to get this, you must be sure it's part of your purchase offer. Once you've made your offer and it's accepted by HUD, it's too late to demand a fix-up allowance.

Bonuses. HUD may also offer special incentives if it's particularly interested in moving a property. For owner-occupants this can include a moving allowance. For investors, this can include a bonus (price reduction) for closing the sale fast. If you have all your financing ducks in a row and can close within a week or two, it can mean a significant financial difference.

Professional Inspections. To avoid buying a "pig in a poke," you'll want to have a professional inspection of the home. However, unlike conventional purchases where the professional inspection is normally conducted after you've signed a purchase agreement with the seller, with HUD you'll need to make your inspection before-hand. HUD doesn't like to tie up homes on contingencies that involve inspections.

As noted, at any given time there are thousands of HUD homes for sale across the country. If you're interested in working the repo part of the foreclosure market, you owe it to yourself to check out the HUD program.

VA

The Department of Veterans Affairs (VA) has an extensive program of loan guarantees. Unlike HUD which *insures* loans to lenders, the VA *guarantees* the performance of a loan to a lender. (Actually, it guarantees only a small percentage of the top of the loan.) If the borrower defaults, the VA pays off its guaranteed portion. How-ever, rather than simply pay out cash, the VA has determined that it is more profitable to actually buy the property from the lender who forecloses and then resell it.

Initially only veterans who qualify (were on active duty during specific time periods) can get VA loans in order to buy a home. After the VA has foreclosed, however, it opens the homes to any-one who wants to buy them, veteran or nonveteran, investor or owner-occupant.

Making an Offer. To purchase a VA home, as with the HUD pro-gram, you must go through a local real estate agent who represents the VA's property management program. Typically these agents will advertise in local newspapers.

You may also find most, but not all, of them listed on the VA's property management Web site. It is up to the local property man-agement office to determine whether to link to the VA site and whether to list its homes on the Web. Check out www.home loans.va.gov/homes.html.

In order to make an actual offer, you must go through an agent and use the proper forms. These include the following:

Offer to Purchase / Contract of Sale (VA form 26-6705)

Credit Statement (VA form 26-6705B)

Financing. The VA will handle financing. However, it prefers to do this only for owner-occupants. And it gives priority to buyers who come in with their own financing (cash to the VA). You'll usually, though not always, do better if you handle your own financing outside the VA.

Condition. As with HUD homes, many of the VA properties are in the same condition as when they were turned over after foreclosure. In the past, however, the VA has had an extensive program of refurbishing properties in order to get a higher market value. If you buy a refurbished home, don't expect to get any kind of bargain on the price. How the homes are handled is largely determined by the regional VA property management office.

Inspections. Again, you'll want to have a professional inspection so that you'll know what you're getting. However, as with HUD, you'll need to conduct the inspection during the offering period and not after you have your offer accepted. The agent who's handling the house can arrange for you and your inspector to get in. Be sure you use a sharp pencil when you calculate how much the property is really worth.

The VA program has been in existence for over 50 years. I've been involved with it at different times and in different ways, and I have seen many owners obtain solid investment property through it.

Fannie Mae

Fannie Mae, along with Freddie Mac discussed next, are the main secondary lenders in the country. They underwrite most of the conventional (non-government-insured or guaranteed) mortgages that are made. What this means is that when you get a mortgage from, say, XYZ lender, it then in effect sells your mortgage to

Fannie Mae or Freddie Mac, for which the lender receives enough money to go out and make additional mortgages.

If, however, you fail to make your mortgage payments and fall into foreclosure, it's Fannie Mae or Freddie Mac (through whatever lender happens to be servicing the mortgage at the time) that takes the property back. Those agencies then have to get rid of it, similar to the way HUD or the VA must dispose of their properties. This, again, can present an opportunity for investors.

Property Types. Fannie Mae underwrites all types of single-family homes, which include detached properties and condos as well as townhomes. Most of their inventory consists of fairly new homes, and often they are in modest to even upscale neighborhoods. My own observation is that the Fannie Mae properties tend to be a little more upscale than either the HUD or VA homes.

Property Locations. As with HUD and the VA, Fannie Mae requires you to go through a local real estate agent. However, the agents are required to list all the homes on the local multiple listing service (MLS), so there's no difficulty in gaining access. Any agent in the local board can show you the home, as well make the offer for you. Your offer will then go to the listing agent who will in turn present it to Fannie Mae.

You can also find a list of Fannie Mae homes at its Web site, www.fanniemae.com/homes.html.

Making an Offer. The transaction is handled just as if you were dealing with any other conventional seller. Fannie Mae can accept, reject, or counter your offer. Indeed, you may go through several rounds of countering before the deal is finally done.

Unlike dealing with either HUD or the VA, you can add contingencies and other conditions with your offer. You may demand to have a professional home inspection *after* the offer is accepted. You can also negotiate over terms, down payment, and financing. Fannie Mae will not, however, accept a contingency that first requires the sale of an existing home.

You may use your own title insurance and escrow company. However, usually in order to have your offer accepted, you must be *preapproved* by a lender. That means that you've had your credit checked and you've had your income and cash on deposit verified.

Condition. These are repos, which means they may (or may not) be in poor condition. Sometimes Fannie Mae will fix up these properties in order to get a higher price. Sometimes they are left in the condition in which they were received. In any event, the homes are all sold in as-is condition, meaning that the buyer must take them with whatever problems they have at the time of sale.

Financing. Fannie Mae does offer its own REO financing. However, it's typically not any better than you get elsewhere. Further, you may have a better chance of getting your offer accepted if you come in with cash to Fannie Mae (secure outside financing).

As with other government repo programs, to get a bargain, you must be on top of the market. You must be able to recognize true value where others miss it. Making a sharp offer can often net you an excellent deal here.

Freddie Mac

As with Fannie Mae, Freddie Mac also offers single-family detached homes and condos and townhomes. However, Freddie Mac generally cleans and fixes up its homes before offering them for sale. If you want to submit an offer on a home doing the fix-up work yourself, chances are that Freddie Mac will still at least clean up the property before you buy it.

Through its HomeSteps program, Freddie Mac will offer homes to owner-occupants at competitive interest rates with 5 percent low down payments and no mortgage insurance. It will also offset some of the title and escrow costs. These homes, however, are almost all competitively priced at market.

Freddie Mac homes are offered through a select group of lenders. To find out more about them, check this Web site: www.homesteps.com.

Other Government Agencies

There are many other government repo programs including some from the IRS as well as local government authorities. Here's a list you may find helpful in checking them out:

> Customs: www.treas.gov/auctions.customs
> Department of Veterans Affairs:
> http://www.homeloans.va.gov/faqmisc.htm
> Federal Deposit Insurance Corporation:
> http://www2.fdic.gov/drrore/index.asp
> GSA: http://propertydisposal.gsa.gov/property/propforsale/
> IRS: www.treas.gov/auctions/irs/real/html
> Small Business Administration:
> http://app1.sba.gov/pfsales/dsp_search.html
> U.S. Marshals Service:
> www.usdoj.gov/marshals/assets/nsl.html
> U.S. Army Corps of Engineers:
> www.sas.usace.army.mil/hapinv/haphomes.htm

TIP You're best off checking these out using the agencies' Web sites. If you call, you could spend hours trying to reach the right person with the correct information. The Web sites, on the other hand, are generally organized to give you the information you need right away.

Buying at Auctions

Nothing determines the true value of a property like an absolute auction.

Why buy a property directly from a seller when you can put in a bid at an auction and hope to get it for a song?

Why indeed? Whenever the price of real estate gets sluggish or falls, auctions appear. (One has to wonder where all the auctioneers go when the market is up?) In a strong real estate market there are virtually no auctioneers. But just let the market slip and they seem to come out of the woodwork.

If you're in an area of the country where the real estate market is slipping, you surely have seen auctions advertised. I'm sure you have also wondered if they are a good deal. Perhaps you've gone to one or two and not bid and still wondered, can I get a really good buy at a real estate auction?

In this chapter we'll look at real estate auctions, the benefits they offer investors, and the pitfalls to avoid. (Note: We're not talking here about buying a property in foreclosure on the courthouse steps as we discussed in the previous chapter. The auctions discussed in this chapter are presumably not for properties in foreclosure.)

We'll take a close look at their appeal and their reality.

TIP Some Web sites such as www.williamsauctions.com and www.foreclosures.com offer online auctions on a regular basis. They're worth checking out.

Commodities Auctions

Auctions as a means of selling a commodity are not new. They're ancient. They are a tried-and-true method of selling dating back to the bazaars of ancient Mesopotamia.

In an auction, ancient or modern, owners of commodities, whether they are jars of olive oil, paintings, or real estate, consign their wares to an auctioneer. The auctioneer, a person skilled in dealing with crowds of buyers, has told the owners that he or she can sell their merchandise for them and get a good price for it. They trust him or her. They put their faith in his or her hands.

As noted, auctions involving real estate are a relatively new phenomenon. Therefore, before looking at them directly, it is instructive to consider auctions in general. We'll do this by looking at an area where auctions have been going on for decades and occur on a regular weekly, even daily basis. I'm speaking of rarities. Rare coin auctions are our example.

An Example of a Commodities Auction. Rare coin auctions are constantly being held by dealers across the country. The dealers advertise the auctions in splashy full-color brochures, in trade papers and in magazines, even on elaborate computer link-ups with other dealers. And, of course, on the Internet.

What they advertise are availability and bargains. A rare coin, like a rare painting, often has many people clamoring for it. The auctions allow the potential buyers to bid one against the other and thus achieve the highest price for the seller. Thus for the seller, liquidity and the possibility of a high price are the big incentives.

But there is a drawback to the seller. What if only one person bids and that is a lowball bid? The rare coin could be sold for a fraction of its true value. To avoid this possibility, most sales are reserve sales. This means that there is a minimum price below which the seller will refuse to sell, the *reserve*. (Often the reserve amount is not announced.)

In reality virtually all auctions are reserve sales. Few sellers are willing to take a chance that due to poor weather or competition from other auctions held elsewhere, or just freak occurrence there will be only a few low bids. Those that do sell without reserve usually live to regret it.

One rare coin dealer whom I know and whose name I won't mention put up a coin conservatively worth $50,000 a few years ago, *without reserve*. It was a bold thing to do and he did it, ostensibly, to draw more people to the auction. When it's without reserve, buyers know they just might get a bargain—buy something for a fraction of its true value. This dealer regretted going without reserve.

The winning bid was $10,000. The coin was sold, and he got $10,000 and lost $40,000. You can be sure he'll never enter a sale without a reserve again.

Of course, from the buyer's perspective, the auction holds out the promise of a bargain. The thought is always present in the buyer's mind that he or she might get a steal. What if you put in a low bid and, for some strange reason, no one else bids? You can get a rare coin for half its real value! You could instantly take it out and resell it at a huge profit.

Hence buyers are more likely to attend auctions that have no reserve. Or auctions where the reserve is not announced and buyers are unaware of its existence. It is the matter of the reserve that is the biggest attraction as well as the biggest stumbling block in the world of auctions.

Real Property Auctions

Real estate auctions are both similar to and different from rarity auctions. For one thing, there's the merchandise. In a rare coin sale (or sale of a painting or other artwork), the owner usually owns the item free and clear. Not so in real estate. Here, the item is almost universally mortgaged. The bank owns most of it.

So what is the owner selling?

He or she is selling equity—that is, his or her equity or interest in the property. (We'll talk about bank auctions shortly.)

This has important consequences for the auction. While in a rare coin auction, the price has at least the potential of falling virtually to zero, at a real estate auction (nonbank), the price can fall only as low as the seller's equity. Below that point he or she doesn't own the property and simply can't afford to sell it.

TIP Most real estate auctions are of two types. In one type there are builders trying to get rid of unsold new homes. In the other, there are lenders trying to dump REOs, often new homes taken back from a builder who was unable to sell them.

Recently there have been occasional auctions where an auctioneer puts together a group of individual sellers, each selling his or her own house. Usually the houses are in close proximity to one another, and the prices are relatively close as well. This is a much more uncommon kind of auction, but one that I would make it a point of attending because it might offer the best opportunity for getting a true bargain.

An Example of a Builder's Auction. Let's consider a typical builder's auction. A builder-developer has put up a "spec" tract of homes. While some have sold, 10 houses remain and, given the real estate climate at the time, cannot easily be sold. So she decides to hold an auction to get rid of them.

The houses have been priced at $500,000 apiece. The builder owes the bank $400,000 apiece. In other words, her equity is $100,000 a house.

The builder hires an auctioneer. The auctioneer places ads in the local papers, inserts 30-second spots on the local radio station, offers the properties on its Web site, and pastes billboards at all the grocery and service stores in the area. Flyers are distributed to local home owners, and special announcements are sent to all the local real estate offices and anyone identified as a potential buyer-investor. All of these announce the day, place, and time of the auction, the property to be auctioned, and the wonderful bargains that are going to be available.

When the auction day arrives and the first house is put up for sale, the auctioneer asks for bids starting at $475,000, which he says is $25,000 less than the previous asking price for the houses.

There are no bids.

The auctioneer drops his price. "Will anyone start out at $465,000? Come on folks, this is a $35,000 bargain!"

Again there are no bids.

The auctioneer looks exasperated and says, "Well, folks, let's go one last time. Will anyone bid $425,000? That's 15 percent off the last asking price for these wonderful homes. Surely someone out there wants to pocket the $75,000 difference?"

Again no bids.

So the auctioneer says, "You know what? Maybe no one wants this house. So let's try the next one."

On and on it goes with the auctioneer eventually getting some bids and probably selling some houses, all above the $400,000 level below which the builder can't go. (For purposes of this example we've overlooked the auctioneer's commission, which comes out of the sales price.)

Note that through clever manipulation the auctioneer never lets the price dip below $400,000. Remember, this was the minimum price at which the builder could sell.

TIP

In many states auctioneers are licensed and are required to announce in advance whether or not there is a reserve price and if there is, what it is.

Absolute Auctions. Not all auctions are like the one described above. Sometimes, particularly in severely depressed real estate markets, "absolute" auctions really are held. These are auctions in which there is *no reserve*. Typically the seller is a lender who holds a clear title to the property after taking it back in foreclosure.

Here, because there is no mortgage holder (the seller being the former mortgage holder), the sales move forward at whatever price is obtained. So the buyer can truly obtain a very low priced property.

The problem, of course, is that absolute auctions are almost always held only when the market is absolutely bad. Typically they involve property that has been vandalized in areas where the crime rate is so bad that no one wants to live there. Often the property has already dropped down close to zero value, so that the seller really doesn't have a whole lot to lose by offering an "absolute" sale.

Thus you, the buyer, typically will come up against two kinds of auctions—the reserve auction that usually involves desirable properties and the absolute auction that typically involves properties that you really don't want.

TRAP

Beware of phony "absolute" auctions. Sellers are well aware that the number of buyers who show up at an *absolute* auction are three times the number who show up at a *reserve* auction. Consequently, a seller might advertise valuable property as an "absolute" sale when it really isn't. This is usually illegal, but it happens.

At these so-called absolute auctions, if the bidding is too low (below the hidden reserve), there always seem to be one or two bidders in the audience who seem to bid the prices higher. Because of these one or two, no properties are sold at a really low price.

Of course, these "bidders" in the audience in actuality may be "shills" (in the parlance of the gambling trade). They may be there to stimulate bidding and also to ensure that no properties are sold at a really low level.

Many states have created laws that prohibit the seller or his or her agents from bidding on property at an absolute auction, the intent being to prevent shills from forcing the price up. In actual practice, however, it's very hard to prove that someone is a shill. The person could be a relative or friend of the seller who, ostensibly, really is interested in buying. So what if a month after the auction the ostensible deal falls through and no sale is made? Who's to know?

In my experience when I see one or two people at a so-called absolute auction preventing the properties from being sold at a low price, I leave. I just have to assume that whether or not it's against the law, some shenanigans are taking place.

Where's the Profit?

Having gone to more than a few auctions in my time, my own experience is that, yes, you can get a deal that's better than the market price. But no, it's usually no better than you could have gotten had you gone directly to the seller yourself and made a lowball offer.

TRAP

Beware of the all hoopla that's often presented at an auction. Sometimes an auction will be held in a beautiful white tent with balloons and streamers. There may be free food and wine tasting. (It should go without saying you should never drink intoxicating beverages while you're conducting real estate or any other kind of business.) The auctioneer and his or her associates may be dressed in tuxedoes. The whole thing may have an upscale "event" beat to it. Don't be fooled. The atmosphere is carefully orchestrated to create a "mob mentality" calculated to make you loosen your wallet and to think that you're getting a great deal, when you're not. It still all comes back to dollars and common sense. The auctioneers can put a washed face on it, but it's still a hard sell.

Auction Terms and Conditions

Auctions almost always specify the terms and conditions under which they operate. While these will differ between auctioneers and states, there are usually several similarities that can be noted.

Deposits

Auctioneers want as many people to attend their auctions as possible, but they want those people to be qualified. Lookers who walk in off the street just to sample the food and drink are not welcome.

Therefore, the auctioneers will often insist that everyone who attends either submit to a credit check beforehand or come with a certified check or cash for a minimum amount of money, often around $5,000. These are your tickets into the auction, and they may actually be collected. The big question that most people ask is, is it refundable?

The answer is yes . . . and no.

At an auction, you're not required to bid. If you put up a deposit and don't bid on a property, you should get the deposit back.

However, I have seen auctions in which the auctioneers suggest that the prices are going to be so phenomenally low that only those who put up a *nonrefundable* deposit will be allowed in to the bidding. In other words, your deposit will be credited toward any purchases you make, but if you fail to make any purchases, you lose it.

It's not clear to me that such a nonrefundable deposit involving real estate is legal in any state. Nevertheless, legal or not, possession is nine-tenths of the law, and if the auctioneer has your $5,000 deposit, it could cost a lot more than that to try to get it back in court.

My suggestion is that unless you have some inside knowledge that convinces you that the auction really will be a barn burner, you should stay away. Simply don't attend any auction for which the deposit is nonrefundable. If possible, never even give the auction company your check until you've made a purchase. (Your good credit should suffice, available by means of a credit report and credit score.) If there's any suggestion that the deposit will be nonrefundable, don't put it up.

On the other hand, what if you are the successful bidder? In that case your deposit is considered earnest money, an actual deposit on the property. If you don't follow through with the purchase, the auction company would be reasonably entitled to keep it.

But what if you don't qualify for the mortgage and can't buy the property, though you want to?

This gets tricky. A lot depends on how the purchase contract that you sign is worded. A good contract will always have a financing contingency that, in essence, says that if you can't get the mortgage and thus can't buy, you get your deposit back. You should carefully read the contract looking for such a financing contingency.

In a bad contract, there probably won't be such a contingency and you could lose the deposit money. Read the contract carefully. It probably is binding.

TRAP

You may agree to contract terms before you actually do the bidding. When you put up your deposit (refundable if you don't bid or aren't successful), the contract you sign may specify under what conditions, if any, the deposit is refundable if you are successful. Read everything you sign and be sure you understand it. Better still, bring your lawyer along to read it (or get it in advance and take it to him or her for an opinion).

Mortgage Preapproval

No one expects you come up with cash when you bid on a real property. It is assumed you'll get a mortgage. Often the auctioneer will help you get it. Sometimes, however, what the auctioneer can arrange might not have as favorable terms as you might be able to handle yourself.

My suggestion is that you get preapproved. Virtually all lenders (including mortgage bankers) are able to do this. It usually just means introducing yourself and providing the credit and income information that is normally given when you apply for a mortgage. Only this time, you provide it before you get the mortgage.

The lender looks you over, financially, and then tells you how big a mortgage you can have, assuming the property qualifies. Be sure that this preapproval is in writing and that it involves a *commitment to lend*. This commitment is all important because it means that when you land the property, you just call up the lender, who arranges for an appraisal, and if the house qualifies, the lender makes the money available for you to buy it.

Other Terms and Conditions

There are a number of other terms and conditions you want to watch out for before you sign anything at an auction. For example, be sure that you are to be given a clear title and that it is backed up by a policy of title insurance. Buying a property with a "clouded" title or one on which someone else has a claim is a can of worms you want to avoid.

Also be sure that there are provisions made for an adequate escrow holder. An *escrow holder* is an independent third party, typically a state-licensed escrow company, that holds your money until the title is transferred. You may end up putting tens of thousands of dollars down, and you don't want to trust this money to the auctioneer or the seller. If they disappear with it, you could have to stand the loss.

Understand the time constraints. Typically you will have only a couple of weeks to get a mortgage and come up with the down payment. In my experience, the auctioneers and the sellers are often willing to extend the time as necessary. After all, they want to make a sale too. But they don't have to, unless it's written into the agreement.

TRAP

Perhaps the worst problem with buying at an auction is that unless you're very knowledgeable about real estate, you're often at the mercy of the auctioneer's and the seller's good intentions. You may need the help of a competent real estate attorney, but you may not have one around when you are required to sign papers that commit you to making a deal or coming up with money.

My suggestion is that if you want to make a bid at an auction, *get expert help!* Hire an attorney who is knowledgeable and experienced and is someone you trust to accompany you and advise you on everything you're asked to sign and do. *Don't rely on the advice of the seller or the auctioneer.* Neither of them is in your corner.

Real estate auctions are two-sided. On the one hand, they can be dangerous. On the other, they can offer great opportunity.

Working the Fixer-Uppers

You can never go wrong in a fixer-upper by paying less. You can always go wrong by paying more.

A *fixer-upper* (or *fixer*) is a property that's in bad shape, bad enough that its condition causes it to sell for a lower-than-market price. Many investors make a career of doing nothing more than buying these fixers, putting them into good shape, and reselling them for a profit. Some investors actually move into fixer homes, repair them, then resell for more than they paid, and then they do it again, stepping their way up to ever more expensive and grander homes.

Whether your plan is to live in a fixer and then resell and buy again, or simply to fix it up and then rent it out, these properties offer good opportunities for those who are handy and who don't mind converting "sweat equity" into profits.

I've done this myself for many years. The best part of this is that it doesn't really matter what the market is like—you can profit in good times and bad. Of course, even more so than with other types of real estate, buying the right property is critical. You can't pay more for the property than its cost plus the fix-up costs plus your markup. If you do, you won't be able to sell for a profit.

TRAP

The biggest mistake that would-be fixer-uppers make is to pay too much for fixer-upper property. It's better to lose a deal or two than to pay too much and end up having to sit on an overexpensive home.

Let's be sure we've got this straight. The cost of the property plus the cost of the fix-up plus your profits can't equal more than the ultimate market price. If they do, you won't be able to sell and get your money out.

TIP

With fixer-uppers it is possible to buy and rent. However, you usually put so much money, time, and effort into the property that you want to resell quickly to get your profits out. My own feeling is that you should not buy deep fixer-uppers if you want to rent. Just buy cosmetically challenged properties, do minimal fix-up, and rent these out.

Where Can I Find Good Fixer-Uppers?

At the outset it's important to understand that unlike most repos and REOs, fixer-uppers can be found in any market and in any neighborhood. You can find them in Beverly Hills and the Bronx. Basically these are properties that the owners have let run down. It might be because of financial considerations, as in a foreclosure. But there might be other reasons as well. Divorce, death, sickness, job transfer—these and other reasons frequently lead owners to stop the upkeep on their properties.

Let a home go for a few months and the landscaping will look terrible. Let it go for a year or two and paint and overall appearance will suffer. Abandon the property and let vandals get in and it will look like a bomb was set off inside. It doesn't take long for a property to skid downhill.

Of course, to paraphrase Shakespeare, "It's an ill wind that blows no man fortune." What you're looking for is the very eyesore that 99 percent of home buyers avoid. You want the house that looks bad, that has exhausted landscaping and paint, that's in terrible condition. You want it so you can buy it for less, fix it up, and sell it for a profit.

Beware of Older Properties

The most commonly available fixer-uppers, and the worst to purchase, are the older homes. I can remember once considering a fixer-upper in Piedmont, an exclusive area of Oakland, California. The house was priced at about two-thirds of the going market value for a house in that neighborhood in good condition. Naturally I was interested. However, what I saw made me turn away.

The house had been built around the turn of the century (the last century!). That meant that it had archaic heating, electrical, and plumbing systems. And they hadn't been much upgraded by previous owners. Of course, it didn't have air-conditioning. I estimated it would take tens of thousands of dollars to modernize the property so that it could be sold at top market value.

But the worst thing was not the obsolescence. It was the termites. The house was entirely wooden. And termites had gotten into the flooring. When you walked on the wooden floors, they gave beneath your feet. Upon examination in the basement, I discovered that not only were the floorboards riddled with termite tunnels but the joists and supporting beams were as well. When I mentioned this to the seller, she replied that she was willing to have the house thoroughly fumigated to get rid of the pests. Yes, fumigation would certainly do that. But what about existing damage to wood?

Good information is the key to working the fixer-upper market. You need to know exactly what's wrong with the property and exactly how much it will take to fix it. If you don't know yourself, it's incumbent upon you to call in professionals who do know and can help you. Don't guess here. Bad guesses will cost you money.

My feeling was that this house was ready to fall down. To my way of thinking, it was a scraper worth just the value of the lot, which was considerably less than the asking price.

All of which is to say that the older the property, the more likely it is to have serious problems that will require costly repairs.

The ideal fixer-upper home will be under 20 years old. That means that virtually all of the problems are likely to be cosmetic— the easiest to fix.

Beware of Problems the Seller Identifies

Sometimes you'll locate a promising property only to be told by the seller (or the seller's agent) that it has a bit of a problem. "Nothing too serious, but something to be considered."

Always be doubly wary when someone tells you the problem isn't too serious. Assume it's *very* serious!

The two most common of the "unserious" problems are a leaking roof and a cracked foundation. If someone identifies these problems in a house you are considering, what exactly are they talking about?

They are talking about money. A new roof costs about $10,000 to $30,000. A new foundation may start at about $25,000 and go up from there.

But, you may argue, can't a roof be patched, a foundation fixed?

Sometimes. But can you tell the difference? With roofs, very often the problem is that the materials have simply worn out. Fix one leak and you'll get three others. This is particularly the case with homes that have roofs over 20 years old. (Another common roofing problem can be bad flashing—the metal that keeps the water out from valleys, around chimneys, and other areas. Finding and fixing the leak can be tricky, though it's usually inexpensive.)

With foundations the biggest problem is ground slippage. The foundation is cracking because the underlying soil is giving way. This can be almost impossible to fix.

On the other hand, maybe it is just a simple leak or a simple foundation crack. If so, it could only cost a few hundred dollars to fix.

The problem to be wary of, however, is when it's identified by the seller. If the seller or agent points out a shifting foundation or a leaky roof, just assume it's a big deal. If it weren't, chances are they wouldn't even bother to mention it.

Cosmetic Fixer-Uppers Can Be the Best

These are the rarest finds. But when one does turn up, it can be a gold mine. Usually what's happened is that there has been a death or divorce in the family. The property may or may not be lived in, but the person who normally would keep it up isn't around. And it has gone downhill.

You can tell a cosmetic fixer-upper because it has certain identifiable features including those listed below.

Features Identifying a Cosmetic Special

1. Spots and stains on the walls
2. Worn, frayed, stained carpeting
3. Broken windows and torn screens
4. Missing or grievously damaged appliances

5. Broken sinks, toilets, tubs, or showers
6. Broken or down fencing around property
7. Yellowed grass and dead landscaping in front and around
8. Doors off hinges (sometimes even the front door!)
9. Holes in yard (where someone tried to bury garbage)
10. Generally depraved condition

After reading all of these features you may think I've misnamed the property. This sounds a lot more than cosmetic!

But it's not. All of the above can be fixed with a little money and lot of attention. Spots and stains on walls and ceilings can be removed simply by repainting. Carpeting can be cleaned or replaced with inexpensive new carpeting. (Cheap new carpeting looks terrific, at least for a while.)

Appliances, sinks, toilets, and other fixtures can all be replaced relatively inexpensively. Doors can be rehung or fixed. Fencing can be straightened, and lawns and shrubs replanted. In short, for a few thousand dollars and some work, the house can be put back into shape.

What a cosmetic fixer-upper does *not* need is a new roof, a new foundation, a new structure, or a new electrical, plumbing, or heating system. You should quickly get the idea that a cosmetic fixer-upper, if it's priced right, is indeed a golden nugget.

TIP

The whole point of finding a cosmetic fixer is to get a good house at a cheap buy. It *looks* so bad that the price is driven down. On the other hand, houses with more serious problems often don't show it. They may be money pits, but they don't *look* bad. Be careful.

Should I Offer Less?

When buying a fixer-upper, there's only one rule: offer less.

Offer much less than the seller is asking. I can almost guarantee that the seller thinks the house is worth more than it is worth. In fact, most sellers want full market price regardless of the condition of the property. Your biggest challenge will be to get them to think realistically and accept a reasonable offer.

Offer less than you think the property is worth. Unless you are very experienced in this field, chances are you will underestimate costs and time required to do work and overestimate what you can get for the fixed-up house. Therefore, after you get to your best estimate of what the work will cost, shave some off of that.

Offer less in counteroffers. Chances are that after you make an offer for less on a fixer-upper, the seller will not accept but instead will counter at a higher price (lower than the asking price but higher than you offered).

The tendency at this point is to want to compromise. Okay, the seller's being reasonable and has come down. So why not be reasonable as well and come up? The reason is you'll end up paying too much. Offer less than you think you should on counteroffers. Yes, you'll miss an occasional good deal. But more often you'll avoid getting in over your head in an overpriced property.

Make the Offer Heavily Contingent

A big problem with buying fixer-uppers is getting all the information together in enough time to make an offer. If it's a hot property, you aren't going to be the only one out there bidding on it. So you probably won't have time to have a plumber, roofer, electrician, soils engineer, or other contractor out to the property to give you an estimate of repairs and cost. (Indeed, you won't want to spend the bucks to get estimates from these people until and unless you have some certainty that you'll get the property.)

So make an offer, but make it contingent on your approving the needed professional inspections. Give it your best shot in terms of price. But then, after you get the property tied up, eliminate the guesswork by having the pros look at the property and tell you exactly what's involved and how much it will cost.

TIP

An inspection approval contingency allows you to back out of the deal (or negoti-ate for a lower price) if you don't approve an inspection report. Typically you have two weeks to conduct the inspections. If you don't like what they say, you're out of there. The only cost is your time and the fees of the inspectors. Be sure a compe-tent agent or attorney draws up the contingency clause so you're protected.

Find Out What the Sellers Really Want

A person who is selling a run-down property is usually a special seller. He or she may be an executor or administrator of a will, a divorcee who wants money fast, or an out-of-state person who needs to get the property off his or her hands. Determine the seller's motivation, and then play to it.

Perhaps the seller needs quick action. If you have already got-ten your financing set, you may be able to offer him or her a three- or even a two-week escrow period. You'll buy for cash (to the seller) and he or she is out of there. That type of offer can mean a lot (in terms of willingness to reduce the price) to many people.

Or maybe your sellers are retirees who want income from earn-ing a good interest rate on their assets and also have their property paid off. Give them an assumable first mortgage at market. They'll love the income and may give you a price reduction to get it. And since the loan is assumable, you can have the rebuyer keep it when you sell. It benefits the original sellers, you, and the rebuyer (who won't have to pay points or expensive loan charges).

TIP

A mortgage at market can carry an interest rate almost twice as high as for a bank deposit. That's a big incentive for sellers with a lot of cash who want income from it: They can earn more from giving a buyer a mortgage than they can from putting their money into a bank account.

How Much Should I Fix?

Fix up only what's necessary. Once you acquire the property, there's a fine line between work that will pay off and work that's wasted time and money. Generally the rule is, do everything that shows. Do nothing that doesn't show.

Of course, in the real world, that's not possible. If the heating and air-conditioning system is broken, you'll have to pay to get it fixed even though the cost will never show up. (The next buyers will just assume that it's in working condition—they won't care a whit that you spent $2,000 to put it that way.)

On the other hand, there may be holes in the walls. Get them patched in a professional way. Give the wall a good coat of texture. And paint it with several coats of high-quality paint. It won't cost that much, and it will show.

Similarly, don't hesitate to put new tile in the entranceway or to replace a badly worn front door. Both will show and will make a difference to a next buyer.

Will Financing Be a Problem?

Lenders won't always go along with your plans for a fixer-upper. They won't like the fact that the property is not in tip-top shape when you purchase it. They will want to lend you less.

That's not necessarily all bad. You can often make a deal with a lender to give you enough money up front to buy the property and then to give you money to fix it up. In this fashion the lender covers most if not all of your costs.

Will lenders do this? You won't know until you ask. Your best sources for this type of financing are *portfolio lenders*. These are banks that keep their own loans (that is, they don't sell them in the secondary market). If you can demonstrate that you're a worthy borrower, they may make this special loan for you—although, of course, it will be at a higher interest rate.

The government also offers similar loan programs. FHA Section 203(k) offers mortgage insurance to lenders (who actually make the loan) on homes that are at least a year old. The mortgage is given in two parts. The first part goes to pay the seller for the purchase. The second part is put into escrow until the property rehabilitation is completed.

These loans will work, particularly if you're living in the home and it's modestly priced. But the loans do have maximum and minimum limitations. You must also submit accurate cost estimates, architectural plans, and other documents, so there is some hassle involved.

However, the value of the mortgage is determined by the property value before rehabilitation plus costs to do the work or 110 percent of the appraised value after rehabilitation (whichever works out to less).

Of course, there are always home equity loans and personal loans, even credit cards. A few investors I know purchase the property in the conventional way and then pay for the rehab work on their credit cards.

When Should I Sell and for How Much?

In Part 4 of this book, we'll discuss in detail how to sell an investment property. However, there are a few challenges specific to fixer-uppers that should be considered here.

First, as touched on earlier, should you rent it out, or should you sell it right after fixing it up?

My own feeling is that it's usually better to sell a property that has been fixed up. For one thing, this gets me past the fixing-up stage. Usually by the time the property's ready to go, I'm sick of working on it. If I rent it out, it means that it will continue to be there with calls from the tenants asking for repairs as they are needed.

Further, at the finish of fix-up time, the property will be in the best shape it's likely to be in for quite a while. Should you use all that spit and polish to attract a tenant, or to attract a buyer? If you rent it out, keep in mind that you'll likely have to go through some refurbishing a second time, when the tenant does eventually move out, in order to make it ready to sell. So why not sell now?

Of course, a lot depends on the market condition. If the market is down, you may well want to hang onto the property for a time until things turn around. Renting, then, would make good sense. On the other hand, if the market's up, then you should be able to get a good price . . . and get out.

If you've done your homework and bought low and kept your rehab expenses in check, you should now be able sell for a healthy profit.

Financing for Investors

The major rule in real estate financing is to use other people's money (OPM) to buy property.

The current new age in real estate financing began a few years ago when mortgage computer profiling came into effect. This new technique makes use of computer technology to create a profile of a successful borrower and a profile of an unsuccessful borrower. By comparing a borrower's credit history to these financial profiles, lenders discovered that they could much more accurately determine who would make the payments and, on the other side, who would default and let their property go into foreclosure.

At first this financial profiling was used exclusively for owner-occupants buying homes. But more recently it has been used for investors. As a result, it is now possible to get much better financing on property you want to buy for investment.

While 90 percent financing for investors is available in some areas, the current standard residential investment mortgage is 75 to 80 percent loan-to-value (LTV). On a $200,000 house the investor must come up with a minimum of $20,000. That's less than half of the previous down payment requirements.

However, even though the new financial profiling system allows lenders to zero in on good payers, they are still loath to give up the old system. Hence, there remains a small interest rate penalty for investors. If you buy to invest, you'll pay a slightly higher interest rate. This is typically expressed in points.

Points: The Bane of Borrowers

As those who are in real estate know, *points* are usually interest prepaid at the time the mortgage is given. Generally, 1 point is equal to 1 percent of a mortgage. For example, 1 point on a $100,000 mortgage is $1,000. If you are charged 2.5 points and are borrowing $200,000, that means you must come up with $5,000. (In actual practice the loan amount is reduced by $5,000—you pay back $200,000 but receive only $195,000.)

TIP

Often you can avoid paying points by agreeing up front to pay a higher interest rate. Points are simply another way of increasing the yield—getting more interest—for the lender. If you agree to an increased interest rate at the outset, the need for points diminishes.

TRAP

When buying residential property, some investors will claim that they intend to live in the property in order to get the slightly lower interest rate and significantly lower down payment offered to owner-occupants. Be forewarned, however, that almost all institutional mortgages are government insured, guaranteed, or repurchased. All of which means that if you're caught, you'll have to answer to the Treasury Department.

Qualifying for an Investment Mortgage

We've already said that getting an investor mortgage involves the same financial profiling system used to qualify owner-occupants. That has to do with how creditworthy you are.

However, there's an additional wrinkle if you intend to buy and rent out the property. There's the matter of having enough income to support the mortgage, according to how lenders calculate such matters. Thus there are two ways that you must qualify: the profile and your income.

Financial Profile Qualifying

The financial profile system works in this manner. In order to get a mortgage, you are given a three-bureau credit check. That means the lender checks out your credit with three national credit checking bureaus: Equifax, TransUnion, and Experion.

This produces a raw credit report, something that you may receive, if you demand it. It will show late payments, bankruptcies, foreclosures, and so on. (Interestingly, it sometimes will *not* show if you are paying your current mortgage on time—I suspect mortgage lenders don't like to let other lenders know who the really good payers are for fear of losing them!)

These raw data are then interpreted by processing the information through a computer program that compares it to other borrowers, both those who have been successful and those who have defaulted on their loans. This is called *financial profiling*. Fannie Mae and Freddie Mac, the two national secondary lenders, use their own system. The Fair Isaac Corporation (FICO) handles the profiling for most other lenders, and it is a private system used extensively to profile borrowers. And the credit bureaus have their own "bankruptcy rating" or other financial profiling systems.

All of these systems take into account your credit habits. For example, if you apply for credit more than three times within a six-month period, using the FICO system, it could have an adverse effect on your rating. (Submitting too many applications suggests that you may be desperate to get money.) Having a large existing mortgage and high borrowing levels on credit cards could adversely affect you in another system. (You're in over your head.) And so on.

You will usually be told your rating. For example, anything over 725 (about the national average) on FICO is usually considered a good credit risk. But you will rarely be allowed to see the actual reasons for your rating. (The lender will send back a note saying why you were denied credit giving a reason, but I've found most of these "reasons" make little sense.) Most rating systems prefer that how they do their work be kept under wraps. The idea is that if consumers (investors in this case) understand how the system works, they'll change their credit habits to get a better rating.

TIP

The trouble with the credit profiling systems is that they may not allow for exceptions. For example, you may have been car shopping and in a single day had credit checks from three dealers. Ultimately, you may not have even bought a car or gotten a car loan. But the checks might still appear, and they could adversely affect your credit. There's really no efficient way of complaining and saying, "Hey, I was just car shopping!"

The upshot is that in order to get the best investor mortgage, you'll need a high credit score. However, getting a lower score will not necessarily eliminate you from a mortgage. It may just mean that you'll pay more points (pay a higher interest rate) to get the same loan.

You can get your credit report free once a year from each credit reporting bureau by contacting www.annualcreditreport.com. You can get your FICO score by contacting www.myfico.com.

Also, you can get individual reports for a fee from these companies:

Experian: www.experian.com
TransUnion: www.transunion.com
Equifax: www.equifax.com

Income Qualifying

In addition to being sufficiently creditworthy to get an institutional investor loan, as described above, you must also have enough outside income. That means that you must make enough money to support the investment.

But, you may argue, the investment is going to support itself. If I buy a rental house, hopefully the rental income will pay for the principal, interest, taxes, and insurance (PITI). That's better than an owner-occupant who will get no income from the property.

So you say. But lenders say otherwise. They want you to qualify for the investment property. And that gets a little bit tricky.

The reason is that you already are living somewhere and are paying rent or mortgage payments. Now when you want to buy an investment property and get an investment loan, your home payments become an expense. If the basic qualifying formula is that income must be three times the payments (the actual formula is close to this), that means you may need much more income to qualify for the investment mortgage.

Not sure why? Let's go over it in a bit more detail.

Let's say your own home mortgage is $1,000 a month. To qualify for it at three times, you need roughly $3,000 a month.

Now let's say you want to buy a rental property with a PITI of also $1,000 a month. Again, you need $3,000 a month in income. But you no longer have $3,000 a month in income because $1,000 of it got subtracted to pay for your home mortgage. Now you need $4,000 a month in income to qualify.

But, you may still be arguing, the rental property produces $1,000 a month in income, so that gets added in and I'm almost back where I started. Ah, if things were only so logical.

Lenders will take into account your rental income, but not all of it. They may only allow 75 percent, in this case $750. They figure the other 25 percent will be lost to vacancies, maintenance, and other expenses.

Further, they'll only allow that $750 to be added to your income, not subtracted from your expenses. Thus, in our example where your total expenses for both properties is $2,000 and you need $4,000 to qualify for the next property, the lenders will subtract that $750 (75 percent of rental income) from the outside income you need to qualify. Now, instead of $3,000 to qualify for that next rental home, you need $3,250 to qualify.

Got it?

If not, just keep in mind that in order to get an institutional investment mortgage, you need to have more income than you need to qualify for an owner-occupant mortgage. Further, the more investment homes you own, the harder it becomes to buy the next one. Each time you need more income to qualify for the next loan!

TIP It's not really so bad. By comparison, in commercial real estate, the investment property itself must produce sufficient income to cover all expenses plus the mortgage payment plus an additional margin for safety.

Buying to Move In and Then Converting

While I've emphasized the importance of being careful not to lie to a lender about your intentions—that is, not to claim you intend to occupy the property when you really don't—what about if you really do?

If you plan to occupy the property, you get a lower down payment (as low as zero percent), a lower interest rate, and easier income qualifying. That's a big incentive to move in. So why not do it?

I've known many investors who over the years have moved regularly from one property to another. They buy, move in, live there for a while, and then convert to a rental. There's no law I know of against it.

The question for many, however, becomes one of how long do you need to live in the property to prove that you really intended to occupy it? I don't know the answer to that. Some people say as little as three months. Others say a year. (Some say it's impossible to prove intent and simply never move in—I suspect you might get away with that argument once, but do it over and over again and someone's going to pull the rug out from under.) It's something you need to check out with your accountant, lawyer, and conscience.

Financing for a Flipped Property

How do you finance a property you intend to flip? Do you need to finance it?

In Chapter 18 we'll discuss the possibility of flipping a property right in escrow so that you never actually take the title. Obviously, in that scenario there's no need for financing.

However, if you do take the title and then quickly resell, say, in six months to a year or so, how do you handle the financing?

My suggestion is that if you're sure that you're going to flip the property and not keep it as a rental, go with any financing you can get. The easiest will probably be some sort of bridge loan (discussed below). If, on the other hand, you want to play it safe and aren't sure you can flip the property, then get long-term financing as discussed above.

Building a Bridge Loan

Bridge loans came into existence to help homeowners purchase a new home while they still had not sold their old home. The loan bridged the gap between the two properties (which is why it is sometimes also called *gap financing*).

A bridge loan allowed the borrower to buy the new property and hold onto it for six months or so until the older property sold. Then, in one scenario, a permanent loan was taken out on the new home.

For our purposes, *bridge financing* means any short-term (six months or less) loan, even a personal loan, that allows us to complete the purchase of the investment property. We don't need a long-term permanent loan because we intend to flip the home.

These short-term loans are available mainly from commercial banks. Typically they will tie up the property as well as your personal assets (in other words, everything in sight!). They are sometimes written at a comparatively high interest rate (or, if you put up other assets, at a comparatively low interest rate, as discussed below).

However, on the other side, they may actually be easier to qualify for. And if you have substantial assets in the bank (a savings account, stocks or bonds you can put up, or other assets), bridge loans may be obtained almost instantly.

Remember, if your goal is flipping, you don't really care about the cost of the mortgage (since it's figured into the expenses of the deal). All you care about is keeping control of the property until you can dispose of it.

An asset-based bridge loan—that is, one that uses the property as collateral—may be just the answer.

Institutional Financing

Yes, institutional financing for investment property is not nearly as good as institutional financing for owner-occupied property. But at least it's available. And that's a real step up compared to only a few years ago.

Seller Financing

In character, the actor Humphrey Bogart once said, "There's three ways of doing things: the right way, the Navy way, and my way!"

Something like this applies to real estate investment financing. Now we're going to look at the last way, creative seller financing.

The traditional, or "right," way to secure financing is to offer a down payment and then get an institutional loan. However, as we saw, this can be expensive and sometimes, depending on your income, next to impossible. So when things become impossible, it's time to do the improbable. And that's to get someone else to handle the financing for you. In most cases, that's the seller.

Short-Term Creative Financing

Here's a plan for only the daring. If you have trouble sleeping at night worrying about money, it's definitely not for you. Furthermore, it assumes that you buy a property and then are quickly able to resell it.

If you're planning to flip a property, you're going to hold it for only a short time. Assuming you don't sell it out of escrow (see Chapter 2), you'll be the owner for only a matter of months (assuming things go as planned). Therefore, why bother to get new financing at all? Why not simply keep the old financing in place?

I can hear previous generations of real estate agents rolling in their graves as I say this because in today's markets, almost no mortgages allow for assumptions. (The exceptions are some adjustable-rate loans, but they require qualifying as if you were getting a new loan.) When you buy a property, the terms of the existing mortgage normally call for it to be paid off in full. In other words, you can't leave the existing financing in place. At least, in theory.

In practice, it's something else.

Let's consider what it is you want out of the financing. Basically, what you want is time—time enough to find another buyer and get the property sold. That's probably going to take you a few months. So how do you buy yourself a few months of time without getting a new mortgage? (Again, this assumes you can't use an option to buy or an assignment, both of which are described in detail in Chapter 18.)

Foreclosure for the Daring?

One risk-taking investor I know dares foreclosure to accomplish this. He gambles that he can sell the property faster than the lender can foreclose. So far, he's been right every time. As noted, I don't advise this technique for the faint of heart! Here's how Jeff does it.

TRAP

The time it takes a lender to foreclose is determined by each state. Usually there are a few months of leeway while the lender contacts the borrower, then there is a notice of default filed, and finally the foreclosure process proceeds to a sale (see Chapter 7). The time involved can be as short as a month or two or as long as a year or more. Check with a good real estate agent and/or attorney in your state to find what the norms are where you live.

Jeff finds a property that he feels is turnable. He does an analysis, and if everything checks out, he makes an offer to the seller in which he agrees to buy the property *subject to* the existing mortgage, meaning that he is neither assuming it nor getting a new loan. Sellers who are desperate to sell in a slow market may very well consider this type of offer.

Buying on subject-to terms has some interesting consequences. It basically means that Jeff is not responsible for the repayment of the existing financing on the property. He agrees to make payments on the mortgage. But if the mortgage goes into foreclosure, it's unlikely to appear on his credit. It will, however, appear on the credit of the original borrower-seller.

Jeff is quite up front about this to the seller. He makes no bones about explaining what he plans to do. Some sellers simply won't go along, worrying that a foreclosure will adversely affect their credit. Others, particularly those highly motivated to sell, usually because of a very poor market, do go along with it.

Jeff explains that the existing financing on the property undoubtedly contains an *alienation clause*, which means that if the title to the property is transferred to another party, the loan immediately becomes due and payable. In others words, the old mortgage can't be assumed without the lender's permission, which normally isn't forthcoming.

So, Jeff explains, he's not going to assume it. He's going to leave it in place and simply try an end run. He'll buy the property subject to the existing loan remaining in place. Then when Jeff resells, hopefully within a few months, the new buyer will get a new loan and pay off the old one, ending the problem.

The difficulty, however, is that if the lender finds out about the title transfer, it could go ahead and demand full payment on the loan—in effect, foreclose.

Sometimes lenders really don't care and are perfectly happy to overlook a title transfer for a mortgage that is performing well, especially in a market where interest rates are steady or falling. Their reasoning is, why replace an existing higher-interest-rate mortgage with a lower-interest-rate one. On the other hand, it's a different story when rates are rising.

Jeff hopes that even if the worst-case scenario occurs, he'll be out of there with a new buyer long before foreclosure can be completed.

Jeff, who's been doing this for some time, also knows that the odds are about 50/50 against the lender's even learning about the transfer.

In virtually all mortgages, when the loan is placed on the property, a reporting company contracts to notify the lender if and when the title to that property has transferred. However, these days, mortgages change hands from one loan-servicing company to another very frequently. It is not uncommon for a borrower to learn that his or her lender of record has changed three times in a single year! As a result, the chances of the current loan servicer discovering a change of title are slight, as long as the payments keep rolling in.

Thus, Jeff figures that as long as he keeps making the payments over the short run, the lender will probably not bother to demand repayment of the mortgage. Of course, if the lender does, then it's a race between Jeff and the time clock to get rid of the property before foreclosure is completed.

TIP

Note that what we are talking about here is simply the triggering (or not triggering) of a mortgage clause with specific consequences spelled out. If a seller sells a house, the mortgage must be paid off. Don't pay off the mortgage and there's the risk of foreclosure. If the seller and buyer are willing to bear the risk and the possible consequences, however, there's little to keep them from proceeding.

Using a Contract of Sale

To further delay any chance of a lender's placing the property into foreclosure, Jeff has taken to not even transferring the title. Rather, he has the sellers give him a *land contract of sale*. This is an old form of transferring property used for years in bare land sales when the buyer couldn't come up with the full purchase price in cash. The seller gave the buyer a contract to buy which said that if and when the buyer ultimately came up with all the cash, the title would be transferred; until then, no cash meant no title. The contract of sale, however, doesn't have to be recorded. (Not recording a change of title is risky for the buyer because the seller could encumber or even sell the property to someone else.)

I don't have any idea how many properties are still transferred today using the contract-of-sale approach, but I wouldn't be surprised if it was in the 5 to 10 percent range. It's typically done for three reasons: The first, just noted, is to give the buyer time to come up with the cash while protecting the seller from giving the title to a property not paid for.

The second is to avoid losing it in the event of a lawsuit. A buyer who is being threatened by lawsuits will sometimes acquire property using a land contract. Since the contract is not recorded, the buyer's name is not on the property, and in a lawsuit that property is less likely to be discovered and become involved.

Finally, a contract of sale is sometimes used in an attempt to circumvent the alienation clause in modern mortgages. Again, since the contract is not recorded, the lender may not learn about the transfer and may not demand that the mortgage be paid.

Most modern mortgages include language stipulating that any transfer, including a contract of sale, is enough to trigger the lender to demand the full repayment of the loan.

The down side to using the contract of sale is that it is a most insecure position for a buyer. If the seller of the property decides that he wants to be dishonest, he can sell it again, even after he has first sold it to Jeff. Since recording of the title is the means by which notice of ownership is established and since Jeff won't be recording the contract of sale, this is possible. A savvy and dishonest seller could do Jeff in. Jeff says the risk is just another cost of doing business.

TIP

In many states a contract of sale can be recorded if at least one party that signs it has that signature notarized.

In risk financing, leaving any existing mortgages in place is an alternative. It can be cheaper, more efficient, and a whole lot easier than trying to get a new institutional mortgage on the property.

TRAP

Don't take a chance with a lender when you're looking at long-term financing— you could get burned. Remember, it's only a possibility because you're trying to move quickly.

"Conventional" Seller Financing

Okay, you may be saying, that takes care of financing a "quicky." But what about when I want to hold and rent out the property? For example, what if a property has an assumable low-balance VA or FHA loan, or what if I can get a new conventional loan for only 75 or 80 percent (LTV) of the purchase price? Can I get the seller to finance my down payment?

Creative financing (or *seller financing*, as it is more appropriately called) came into vogue in the 1950s. At that time the mortgage market was entirely different from what it is today. Virtually all residential mortgages were offered by savings and loan associations. And those organizations wanted to keep their loans in place. (They wanted to avoid the thousands it cost to replace a mortgage when a borrower paid off his or her loan.) So they made all of those mortgages assumable. They wanted them assumed!

Indeed, there was almost always a penalty for paying them off early. Typically if you paid more than 20 percent of your mortgage in any year, there was a penalty of six months' interest—a very heavy hit.

As a consequence, when people bought properties, rather than get new financing, they kept the existing loans. But that practice produced a problem of a different sort. As prices rose, the difference between the old loan and the new price increased, meaning that buyers had to come up with larger down payments. And if there's one thing that buyers have trouble doing, it's coming up with bigger down payments.

As a consequence, creative, or seller, financing came into vogue. The seller would give to the buyer a second mortgage for 20 percent or more of the purchase price. Perhaps an example will help here:

Example of Typical Old-Fashioned Seller Financing	
Seller financing second mortgage:	$30,000 (new)
Existing mortgage:	+ $70,000 (assumable)
Sales price:	$100,000

In the above example, the seller has an existing assumable mortgage of $70,000 and a sales price of $100,000. That means the buyer must come up with the difference of $30,000.

However, there are very few buyers who can put 30 percent down. So the seller *carries the paper* for $30,000, and the buyer needs to come up with only the closing costs.

That's how it was done in the 1950s and 1960s.

But then in the 1970s inflation came roaring out, and lenders wanted to call in all those old low-interest existing assumable loans and replace them with high-paying high-interest loans. So they did away with assumptions, and that's where we are today.

But creative financing (or seller financing) still exists if you want to use it. It can be a way for the buyer to borrow most or even all of the down payment. It works the same way as in the old days.

Instead of giving the seller a cash down payment, you have the seller carry the financing. How much the seller will carry depends on what agreement you reach. You might put down 10 percent cash. Or 5 percent cash. Or even nothing. It all depends on what you both agree upon.

And instead of assuming an existing loan, in most cases you get a new institutional first mortgage. Now the financing looks like this:

Example of No-Down-Payment, Modern Seller Financing

Seller financing second mortgage:	$30,000 (new)
New first mortgage:	+ $170,000
Sales price:	$200,000

TIP

In the 1980s, creative financing got a bad name because unscrupulous buyers bought property with nothing down using seller financing and then never made a payment and ultimately let the properties go. The sellers were forced to foreclose to protect their investment, and they often ended up with little to nothing. Hence, today it's less likely you'll find a seller willing to accept creative financing and nothing down. More likely the seller will want you to put at least 10 percent down.

Example of Low-Down-Payment, Modern Seller Financing

Down payment:	$20,000
Seller financing second mortgage:	$20,000 (new)
New first mortgage:	+ $160,000
Sales price:	$200,000

Assumable Mortgages. As noted, there are still some older existing VA and FHA loans out there that are assumable. However, they typically have a very low balance. The advantage, of course, is that there is little to no qualifying here. So someone with terrible credit can make a purchase.

With seller financing, the seller must come up with a bigger second mortgage:

Example of Modern Assumable Seller Financing	
Down payment:	$20,000
Seller financing second mortgage:	$80,000 (new)
Assumable first mortgage:	+ $100,000 (old)
Sales price:	$200,000

The advantage here is that you can assume the existing mortgage without qualifying along with its presumably low interest rate and low monthly payments. Further, you don't need to worry about the lender trying to accelerate the mortgage (foreclose) because the loan is assumable (and you assume it).

TRAP

Just because a mortgage is old, it doesn't mean that the interest rate is low. Some older mortgages had high interest rates. It's something to check out.

Finding a Paid-Off House. A final alternative for seller financing is to find a paid-off property. If the sellers don't owe anything, they may be willing to give you a new mortgage for close to the full amount of the purchase price. Even if they owe a small amount, they may be willing to pay this off with your down payment and give you a new mortgage themselves.

Why would sellers do this? If they are older and want to retire, the thought of receiving regular income from a relatively high interest rate mortgage (when compared to the low bank interest rates they would be paid on savings accounts or CDs) can be quite appealing. Further, since it's a first mortgage, it's fairly secure.

TIP

Make sure that any new mortgage that the sellers give to you is fully assumable. That way, you can use it to help the next buyer take over the property. If the sellers balk at full assumability, have it written as *one time assumable*. That way you can have it assumed by your rebuyer, and you can get out of the property.

With the increase in availability of institutional mortgages today (more appealing, as we saw earlier, to investors), creative financing has almost been forgotten. But don't you forget about it. It can be an excellent way of buying investor property with little down. And if your intention is to flip without using an option to buy or an assignment, it can provide just the answers you need to gain control of the property and hold it for just long enough to get a rebuyer to take it over.

Renting

It's Harder . . . and Easier . . . Than You Think

You can't expect to be a successful real estate investor without spending some time as a rent collector.

Being a landlord goes with the territory when you invest in real estate. It's your basic means of generating income from the property. (Your other alternatives are to refinance or to sell.)

For many people becoming a landlord comes naturally. For others, it's difficult and strange. For all of us involved in property ownership, however, it's necessary that we learn how to do it and how to do it well.

My memories of my first experiences at landlording are still vivid. I was 18 years old, and I was collecting rent from tenants in a triplex (three units in a single structure). I was there every week and sometimes more than once a week inquiring if there was anything the tenants needed, mowing lawns, painting, making sure the plumbing and heating worked well, and on and on.

I made it a point to show up right on the day rent was due to collect, and if a tenant was late, I immediately served a three-day notice to pay or quit. If the tenant still didn't pay, I immediately began eviction proceedings. I wanted my rent when it was due, no excuses!

Looking back on it, I realize I was a terrible landlord. I smothered my tenants with too much attention. And then I wasn't flexible enough when they had real problems.

Further, I probably spent 20 hours a week nursing that triplex along. I couldn't have been making more than a few dollars an hour given the time and effort I put forth.

Now, of course, I realize that most of what I did was superfluous and unnecessary. If I had been willing to let the rent ride a few days to a week, I probably could have avoided nearly all my threats of eviction. I was an overly zealous landlord.

It could be argued that this is better than being too lax. Some landlords never show up at the property, don't fix things when they break, let the rent lapse for weeks and sometimes months—in other words, they simply don't take care of their rentals.

When you're a landlord, you don't want to do too much . . . or too little. In a sense, taking care of rentals is a bit more like an art than a science.

It's Business, Not Personal

One thing that's helpful to keep in mind is that when you're a landlord, you're in a much more financially demanding position than the tenant. As the landlord, you own the property. You stand to reap all the profits if values go up and to lose a significant amount of money if they go down. You also have all the responsibilities of paying the taxes, insurance, and mortgage as well as paying for repairs. The tenant has none of those responsibilities. He or she only has to get the rent in on time and keep the place reasonably clean and tidy.

Because of the different responsibilities, you can never be on the same level as the tenant. The property is always going to mean more to you than it does to the tenant. And you are always going to have to be in the position of having to hold tenants to the terms of tenancy they agreed to.

In short, renting property is not democracy in action. It's a business. You're more like a CEO and the tenant is more like an employee.

While this analogy is helpful, it's important not to stretch it too far. To counter tyrannical and unfair treatment by some landlords, the courts over the years have strengthened tenants' rights to the point where today many landlords feel the tenants have the upper hand. In most states the landlord is so restricted in what he or she can or can't do that some people say it just isn't worth renting out property any more.

I don't find that to be true. To my way of thinking, the courts and the legislatures have simply given tenants protections that they needed from unscrupulous landlords. If you're not unscrupulous, you should have little to worry about.

The whole point of this discussion is to note the importance of striking the right tone in your relationship with a tenant. You can't be arbitrary or dictatorial. Yet you can't be a wimp either.

You have to be in charge. It's your property, and how you handle the tenant will largely determine what happens to it. Get your head straight. The tenant is not doing you a favor by renting from you—he or she needs shelter and has to rent from someone. On the other hand, you're not doing the tenant a favor—there are lots of other rentals.

Remember, it's a business and should be run as such. You're the boss, and within the law, you set up the rules and see that they are followed. Keep to that thinking and you should do well.

TIP

Before you begin your tenure as a landlord, pick up a set of landlord and tenant laws appropriate to your state and study it thoroughly. While the rules may differ from state to state, in almost all cases they are plain, and you don't want to break them. A tenant lawsuit is no fun for anyone.

A Typical Progression into Landlording

Here's how most investors get involved as landlords. It's a learn-as-you-earn approach, and it has many advantages.

The First Property

Typically the first investment property is a single-family house or a condo. This is the easiest to deal with as a landlord because you only have one tenant.

The first-time landlord begins by fixing up the property—painting, cleaning, and putting it into tip-top shape.

TRAP

A rental does *not* need to be in as good a shape as a property up for sale. It needs to be clean, even spotless, but it does not need new carpeting, new appliances, made-over kitchen and bathrooms, and so on. Don't make the mistake of spending a lot of money preparing a property for sale and then renting it out.

Then there's advertising for a tenant in the local newspaper, on bulletin boards, on *local* Internet sites, and so on. When would-be tenants call, there's running out to the property to show it. And when prospects express interest, there's having them fill out applications.

TRAP

Be sure to give all prospective tenants an application. You don't want to be guilty of violating any antidiscrimination laws.

It's at this point that the new landlord typically begins learning about many of the laws and rules that affect landlord and tenant relations. You should consult with an attorney in the area who can present local, state, and national rules in the following areas.

Areas of Landlord-Tenant Laws and Regulations

- Antidiscrimination
- Taking and holding deposits
- Making disclosures about lead and other substances in the building
- Fire and safety guidelines

There are probably additional areas of rules and laws that apply in your state or municipality.

When I first began renting property, landlords simply went out and did it. Today, you would be foolish to attempt to rent property unless and until you understood and followed all the legal guidelines. And keep in mind that while some of the rules, laws, and guidelines are national in scope, others are state and even locally mandated. Thus, what's true for one area may or may not be true for another.

When a prospective tenant shows up who wants to rent, the new landlord should (with the tenant's written permission) get a credit report and check with previous landlords. This is done to get a clearer picture of the would-be tenant's track record and financial strength.

Then, a decision has to be made: Will this prospect make a good tenant?

TIP

Remember, you can't turn a tenant applicant down because he or she has children or because of his or her race, religion, national origin, most health issues, sexual preference, or any other characteristic or status that has special protection. You can, however, turn him or her down for strictly financial considerations, as long as you apply these fairly and equally to all prospects.

If you decide to rent, you have to determine whether your terms will be month to month—whereby either you or the tenant can terminate the rental with 30 to 60 days' notice—or year to year by means of a lease—whereby both you and the tenant are locked in for a longer period of time, typically a year but sometimes six months.

Most new landlords like the idea of a long-term lease because it presumably means he or she won't have to worry for at least a year about rerenting the property and all that it entails, such as cleaning up, advertising, and showing it to prospective tenants. However, I find a lease a bad idea. It locks the landlord into a specific rent that cannot normally be raised during the lease period. Also, having a lease-holding tenant can make it more difficult to sell the property. And finally, if the tenant refuses to pay the rent and leaves, the only way you can collect on the lease is by suing each month as the rent comes due (and often the tenant has flown the area and can't be found).

Think twice before insisting on a lease instead of a month-to-month arrangement.

TIP

With month-to-month terms, you can usually insist on a big cleaning deposit and in many areas a security deposit as well.

Once the place is rented out, the first-time landlord typically thinks things will settle down. And sometimes they do. However, other times it becomes a matter of going out to the rental whenever the tenant calls. The reason for the calls can be anything from a leaking faucet to a broken water heater to a neighbor's dog that barks all night.

As a new landlord, you'll want to fix these issues. Some you'll be able to deal with directly. (It's helpful if you can handle minor plumbing and electrical issues yourself; however, beware of doing any major work that could involve liability if something goes wrong and injures the tenant.) Others, like a barking dog, you may be able to handle only peripherally, such as by nicely asking the neighbor to quiet the animal. Or calling the police department. (Both of these measures may or may not solve the problem.)

If you're lucky, the calls will diminish after a while, and then you'll simply need to check your rental once a month . . . until the tenant moves out and you have to start all over again.

Multiple Properties

Typically investors will soon buy a second rental property, and then a third, and then perhaps a multiple-unit dwelling (an apartment building), and on and on. It's not uncommon for the successful investor after a decade in the business to have between 12 and 20 rentals.

Does that seem like an overwhelming number of properties to take care of?

Think of the story of the boy whose farmer father gave him a calf right after it was born. Each day the boy would lift the small calf, which weighed very little.

But the calf grew, as did the boy. Over time and years the boy was lifting a heifer that weighed over a hundred pounds. And as the years passed, he was lifting a cow that weighed hundreds of pounds.

If the boy had started out trying to lift the cow when it was close to full grown, it would have been far too heavy a burden to handle. But by lifting it when it was small and then continuing to lift it each day as it grew heavier and heavier, the boy didn't really notice the increase in weight . . . until he was lifting what to someone else might have seemed an impossible weight.

The same thing happens with rentals. When you start out small, with one rental, you slowly learn how to deal with it. You learn how to handle tenants, what to clean, what kind of rental agreements to use, when to let the rent slide for a week and when to evict, and on and on.

Then you take on a second rental, and the knowledge you have gained from the first allows you to easily handle both.

Then you get another . . . and another. Until, over the years, you're handling dozens.

Could you have started out successfully managing a dozen or more properties? Almost certainly not.

Can you learn to do it over time? Almost certainly you can.

Which is why I always suggest starting off slowly and building up to increasing numbers of rentals. Yes, you can learn a lot about how to be a landlord from books, from talking with agents and attorneys, and from other sources. But there's no substitute for personal experience. And that only comes with time.

As noted at the beginning of the chapter, if you want to be a successful investor in real estate, you're going to have to get into it with both hands. And that means becoming a landlord and renting out property. The next chapters will give you some important tips on getting off to a fast start . . . and maintaining a true course along the way.

Valuating Property for Rental Potential

It doesn't matter what you paid, what you owe, or how much you have into the property. It only matters what the market will bear.

Surprising to many newcomers, not every property will make a good rental. Some properties are perfect as rentals, some are absolutely hopeless, and most fall somewhere in between.

In this chapter we're going to consider what makes a property the right choice for a rental. Presumably, you'll want to buy these (unless you're planning on flipping) and avoid the others.

Location Tripled

It's a truism that wherever there are people, you can rent out a home. However, some areas are better for rentals than others. Ideally you want your investment property to be in a good rental area. You want to be able to get a high rental rate and be able to rent out the property quickly and keep it rented. That's how to maximize your rental income.

What makes a good rental area? It's one in which there are many highly salaried tenants available. Typically this is an area where there's lots of commerce and industry providing jobs.

However, you want to be sure that your rental matches the types of jobs available. For example, if there's a manufacturing plant in town that provides a lot of stable blue-collar workers who can afford to pay up to $1,000 a month in rent, a property that you can rent for under $1,000 a month (and still pay your expenses) would be a sound investment.

In contrast, a property that you needed to rent for $2,000 a month to make expenses would make little sense in this area. You'd have nothing but long periods of vacancy.

On the other hand, perhaps in another community there's an industrial park that provides lots of high-paying white-collar workers who can easily afford to make $2,000-a-month payments. Now your home with the $2,000 rental makes good sense. In fact, you might actually have trouble renting out a home for only $1,000—it might be too small or lack features that the higher-paying tenant population is demanding.

In other words, your rental property must be suited to the market in which it's located.

How Do I Determine the Local Market?

There are two ways to accomplish this: the hard way and the easy. The hard way is to spend some time investigating the area. Check with the local chamber of commerce for the types of employers in the area. Then call on those employers to find out what kinds of tenants they are likely to offer.

You can do that. Or you can call a few real estate agents who specialize in property management and just ask. In a few sentences they should be able to tell you what the market's like. Further, if you have a particular house (or other property) in question, they should be able to give you a fairly accurate estimate of just how much you can rent it for. This is particularly the case if they are farming the area (know it very well). Keep in mind, of course, that they're hoping to sign you up as a client.

Can you rely on such word-of-mouth opinions? I have. But to be sure, check the local newspaper rental section. The rental ads are always divided up by area. Find the area your subject home is in and call a few landlords. Find out what they're offering and how much they're charging. You should be able to get a conclusive answer within three or four calls.

TIP

When you look at rental ads, also look for how many there are. A huge number of ads suggest that perhaps there are too many rentals (or not enough renters) in your area.

How Do I Know If the House Will Make a Good Rental?

What you need to look for is a property without too many angles. By "angles" I mean items that require tender loving care (TLC). You want a property that will pretty much run itself because if there's one thing you can count on, it's that most tenants won't give the property TLC.

Avoid Older Properties

Older homes need more care. Here's a list of problems that you, and your tenants, are likely to run into in older homes.

Problems of Older Homes

- *Plumbing distress* from leaking faucets (which you have to run out and fix) to leaking pipes (which require moving the tenant out while the house is replumbed).
- *Electrical distress* from light switches and plugs that suddenly burn out (which you have to run out and fix) to overloaded circuits that if not fixed can threaten fire. Older homes tend to have wiring that's too lightweight for today's modern appliances. Tenants can easily overload the wiring by plugging too many heaters, lights, washers, or whatever into the same circuit, blowing fuses and circuit breakers. All of which can necessitate expensive rewiring.
- *Roof leaks* might cause an owner to put up with a bucket for a while, but a tenant will want a leak fixed instantly.
- *Worn-out appliances* may be kept running by an owner for a few years by tenderly caring for them, but tenants will simply turn them on full, and if they don't work, expect instant replacements.
- *System problems* from termites in the floor to bad heaters and air-conditioning. If you're in the place, you can tolerate it for a while, perhaps even doing some of the repair or replacement work yourself. If it's a tenant, the repairs will have to be done immediately, or you'll lose the tenant . . . and your rent.

A new house, preferably one less than 25 years old and ideally less than 10 years old, is not apt to have such problems. Newer properties have newer plumbing, electrical systems, roofs, appliances, and air-conditioning systems. So there is far less chance that anything expensive will need to be completely replaced.

Avoid Condos

Many people like the idea of buying a condo as a rental because the initial investment is usually lower than for a house. And while some people do successfully rent condos for years, overall I feel they make bad rentals.

The reason is the homeowners association (HOA). All condos are part of an HOA including any you'll buy. And the HOA will set the rules for everything from changes you can make to the exterior to noise in the evening to where cars can be parked.

In other words, there are lots of rules. And while owners tend to follow these rules, if reluctantly, because they realize the purpose of the rules is to keep up the overall value of the property, tenants have no such constraints. Tenants could care less about property values since they don't own the property. Hence, when renting a condo expect all sorts of continuing problems with the HOA. Expect your neighbor owners to complain at the drop of a hat about your tenants' activities. And expect to be fined and chastised by the HOA over what your tenants do. It's just so much hassle that it's often not worth it.

Of course, as I say, some landlords do rent condos successfully. But then again, there are some people who are willing to put their heads into a lion's mouth.

For more information on condos and co-ops, check my book *Tips and Traps When Buying a Condo, Co-Op, or Townhouse* (McGraw-Hill, 2006).

TIP

Doubly avoid trying to rent out co-ops. The control from the board is far deeper and more relentless than it would be even from a condo HOA. Indeed, many co-op boards will have the right, based on strict financial criteria the boards apply to applicants, to veto any tenants you may want. (Sometimes, though not allowed by antidiscrimination laws, a co-op board may require tenants to meet personal qualifications as well.)

Avoid Homes with Lots of Bedrooms

The problem is that the higher the number of people that occupy the property, the more wear and tear (and potentially damage) there will be to it. This goes double for children, who in their play tend to bump, dent, gouge, and even chew up walls, floors, doors, and other building fixtures.

The old adage from landlords years ago used to be, "I love children, in your place, not mine!" However, antidiscrimination laws prohibit you from refusing to rent to a family because it has children. You can, however, refuse to rent if the home is too small to accommodate the family. Therein lies the reason for not having too many bedrooms. Be aware, however, that the number of children allowed in a bedroom according to HUD (Housing and Urban Development) and most fire departments is quite large.

TIP

The fewer the bedrooms, the fewer the number of tenants, and as a result, the less wear and tear to the property.

While I've never found a hard-and-fast rule that stipulates the maximum number of people that can occupy a bedroom (some fire regulations put it at four!), it's a cinch that the more bedrooms you have, the more people you will have occupying the property. It stands to reason that a house with four bedrooms can have more people in it than a house with only one, even if both properties have the same square footage.

Does that mean that a one-bedroom house makes a good rental? Not usually. You won't find many tenants (or many buyers, subsequently) that want only one bedroom. But two- and three-bedroom properties do make good rentals. And, in my opinion, four- and five-bedroom properties most certainly do not.

Avoid Big Lots

If you're the sort of person who likes room to roam, then buy a house with a big lot to live in. But if you're an investor, avoid houses with big lots like the plague.

A big lot requires big maintenance. If it's got lots of lawn and landscaping, you'll need to hire (and pay for) a gardener to take care of it. You can't count on the tenants to do that.

In the West and Southwest, look for automatic sprinklers in any rental. If the rental **TIP**
doesn't have a watering system, put it in. If the system isn't automatic, upgrade it.
Don't count on a tenant to take care of watering for you. An automatic system,
however, should do the job.

The bigger the lot, the more upkeep involved. Furthermore, when it comes time to resell, you'll find that a big lot will only marginally return any more money to you. In some markets, it may actually get a reduced price!

Avoid Homes with Pools

There are two reasons: upkeep and liability. Until you have a pool, you can't believe how much upkeep it requires to ensure that it's clean and swimmable. Let a pool go and you'll find that algae very quickly destroy the plaster and filters, that equipment deteriorates, and that bringing it back up to par, if even possible, can be very costly.

A pool is also a big liability headache. There's always the chance that someone could fall in and be seriously injured or even worse, could drown. To protect yourself, you'll need at least a five-foot fence with a self-closing gate all the way around the pool. And you'll need to rely on your tenants to maintain the fence and gate.

And even if the pool is protected, unless the water is properly filtered and cleaned, there's always the danger that a swimmer could get sick from swimming in it. You can be sure that if this happens and there's a lawsuit, you will be held liable as the owner-investor.

TIP

It goes without saying that if you buy a rental with a pool, you'll want to carry a big liability insurance policy. The bigger the better, but I would never get less than $3 million. And this can also get expensive.

Always hire a pool service to maintain the pool. Don't rely on tenants to do this. Even if they want to, they often forget or do something incorrect that ends up costing you even more money.

How Do I Know If the House Is in Rental Condition?

A clean home will rent quickly to a clean tenant. But to sell a home, it will need to be more than just clean. It will have to look new.

If you fix up a property to rent, you need to go only so far. Get it clean and you'll find a good tenant.

However, if you fix up a property to sell, you need to go much further. You'll need to paint everywhere, recarpet, replace appliances, cabinets, and countertops, do kitchen and bathroom makeovers, and so forth.

Therefore, when buying a property that you plan to rent out, you don't need to look for a property that's been upgraded and is spotless. It needs only to be serviceable and clean. And this should be reflected in a more reasonable price.

On the other hand, if the property you're considering has been fixed up to sell, chances are the seller has spent a great deal of time, money, and effort on it. And this will be reflected in a higher price.

But as an investor looking to rent out a home, you don't really care about that extra effort made to bring the home up to selling condition. You're more interested in a lower price.

Therefore, don't pay for a Cadillac when you need only a Chevy. Don't buy a home for a rental that's been primped for sale. You're throwing your money away.

Of course, you can always rent a thoroughly fixed up home to tenants. However, chances are those tenants over the course of a few years will bring that home down to rental condition. By the time you're ready to resell years later, the home will still need reconditioning.

How Do I Judge the Direction of the Economy?

When buying a property for investment, you'd be in error not to take into consideration the local economy. You could do everything else right and still be tripped up by a bad market.

There are really only two things you need consider from the perspective of the rental market and the economy. The first is whether times are good or bad in the area. The second is the demand for housing in your area.

Put simply, when the economy is booming, lots of people have jobs and can afford to rent. In a booming economy, you'll do well buying a rental property.

TRAP

Keep in mind that the economy is not homogenous. While nationally it may be doing well, it could be doing badly in your area. Be sure you check the economy where you plan on buying your rental investment.

The second consideration is the supply and demand for housing. You want big demand, small supply. When it's the other way around, it's an indication not to buy an investment home.

Most areas of the country have long had a shortage of housing. The simple rule is to buy when and where the economy is good and the housing market is tight.

How do you know? Just read the local newspapers. You can count on articles detailing information on this at least once a week and sometimes every few days.

For a quicker answer, check with a local real estate board. They keep statistics on such things and can usually give you a quick answer. Look for the amount of unsold inventory and the number of houses listed "for rent." A local college with a real estate department is another good source.

When you buy an investment property that you need to rent out, make your purchase wisely. Check out the location, the type of home, its condition, and the economy. Only when all say "go" should you make the leap.

The Basic Rules for Being a Successful Landlord

It's a business like any other. If you let the tenant make his problem, into your problem, you've lost the game.

Some people live and work by rules. Others play it by the seat of their pants. Either way can work fine—it's just a matter of style.

However, no matter what your approach, it's helpful to have some guidelines to show the way. Here are those that I have found most helpful.

Rule 1. Offer a Clean Rental

The Biblical observation "As you sow, so shall you reap" really does apply here. If the property you rent is clean when the tenant moves in, the chances are very good it will be clean when the tenant moves out.

This should be obvious, but it really isn't. I have known many landlords who really don't care what their property looks like. Their attitude seems to be, "I'm not going to live there, so what do I care? Let the tenants clean it if they want!"

That's not a very charitable attitude, and it often comes from having a tenant who leaves the property a mess. However, having once been burned does not mean you need to fear fire. Dirty and messy properties take far longer to rent, command lower rents, and attract a much lower-quality tenant. The person you really hurt when you fail to clean up your rental is you.

I always go through a rental and clean the carpets and floors, and I make sure the kitchen is spotless with the stove, refrigerator (if any), and the sink shiny and clean. I also repaint the walls as necessary. When prospective tenants walk in, I want them to think they are getting a place that's as clean as new. That way, hopefully, they'll take pride in living there and will take care of it.

Sometimes when a property has a lot of tenants moving through it, it begins to take on a shabby appearance. After a while the landlord tires of spending the money and time to clean it after each tenant and instead, offers to pay for the paint and cleaning equipment if the tenant will do the clean-up work. This works only in a very limited way. If the property is already cleaned up but a little bit on the worn side and the tenant wants a gallon of paint to touch up a bedroom, by all means consider buying the paint. (Beware of tenants who can't paint and do a messy job!) You probably have a very clean tenant who will take good care of the property.

On the other hand, if the place is a mess and the tenant wants a gallon of paint to fix it up, don't buy the paint. Have the place fixed up before you go looking for a tenant.

I've tried it both ways, and I've found that tenants who are willing to rent a place that is a mess, even if they are willing to clean it up a bit, will still turn out to be poor-quality tenants who have trouble making rent payments and who leave the place even worse.

A good tenant simply won't accept a rental that's a mess. He or she won't want to spend much time (with the occasional exception of the fastidious tenant noted above) cleaning. They know they are good tenants, they know they can find a clean place, and they will skip yours. As a result, you get what's left—the type of tenant you don't want.

TIP

If you do buy paint for the tenant or otherwise allow the tenant to fix up the place, be sure that you choose the paint, wallpaper, or whatever. Always select the best possible quality (so it will last) and the most generic colors (so they will appeal to the most people). If you let the tenant make the selection, you could end up with a purple bathroom and red living room.

Rule 2. Pay the Water Bill

In most rentals the tenant pays the utility bills. This includes gas or oil, electricity, phone, and water. This is almost certainly the case with single-family residences where everything is separately metered and is often the case with apartment buildings where each unit is individually metered.

There's nothing wrong with this, unless you live in an arid climate and have a lot of landscaping. That landscaping will take water and in arid climates, water tends to be expensive. Don't expect any tenant to go out of his or her way to pay a big water bill to help your landscaping. Yes, most tenants do like nice landscaping. No, most tenants won't pay extra for it.

The answer is a water allowance. It doesn't have to be much. It doesn't even have to equal the costs the tenant will pay for all water actually used. It's just the idea that you're contributing. Each time the tenant thinks about not watering, he or she will remember that allowance, not get angry about the cost, and will water.

It doesn't work for every tenant, but it does work for many, and it could save you a lot of costs in relandscaping later on.

TIP If you have large yards in front and back, you may want to consider providing a gardener. You often can charge more rent with a gardener, so there could be almost no cost to you, and it can mean keeping the property in great shape. If the property has a pool, a pool maintenance service is a must. Never rely on a tenant to take care of a pool. If the tenant lets it go, it could cost thousands to bring it back into shape—far more than the minimal monthly charge for a professional service.

Rule 3. Know the People You're Renting To

As suggested earlier, the way to get a tenant to take care of the property and pay the rent on time is to rent to the right tenant in the beginning. This is the biggest problem area for most new landlords—getting the right tenant. How do you do it?

Rest assured there is no guaranteed formula. There are, however, certain tips that can prove helpful.

Of course, you will want to talk with the prospective tenants and form an opinion of them. (This is very important and why I always suggest that you do the renting up of the property personally.) Here are two critical areas to consider.

The Credit Report

Today, you as a landlord should have no trouble getting a written credit report on a prospective tenant. All that you really need to do is contact one of the local apartment owners associations (listed in your phone book), explain what you want, and possibly join up (a really good idea). They should have the credit reporting forms. The cost is usually under $25 for a brief report. You can also go online to: www.tenantverification.com or www.e-renter.com.

When you find likely tenant candidates, have them fill out the form, *being sure they give you permission to check their credit history.* Then submit the form. Usually within a day you'll have a printout of the applicant's credit history. (You may even get a credit score included.) Check it over carefully.

Ideally you're looking for tenants with no bad credit. They pay all their bills on time and have credit with a wide variety of lenders from credit card companies to department stores to banks. Chances are, however, you won't find this kind of tenant all the time (or even very often). More likely the person who rents has spotty credit—some good, some bad.

Study the credit report. If the prospective tenants have a lot of "late-paying" notes, chances are your rent won't be paid on time either. If they have some loan defaults or other failures to pay, you may not get your rent at all.

The credit report should be taken as an indication of how the prospective tenants view their credit. If they view it casually and don't really care, then you could end up with no rent. You want tenants who take their credit seriously and who regularly pay on time. One of the biggest mistakes is to "fall in love" with a tenant (not literally, but figuratively). The tenant seems ideal, until the credit report comes in. You look at the bad credit report and then choose to ignore it because you're so convinced the tenant is wonderful. Bad move.

Ultimately it's a judgment call. Just remember, however, that if you decide not to give a bad credit report a lot of credence, then why did you order the credit report in the first place?

Give the tenant a chance to explain bad credit. Listen to the explanation. It may be perfectly logical and may not be the tenant's fault.

The Previous Landlord's Recommendation

To me this is the single most important indicator of future tenant success. It's absolutely vital that you get the accurate name and phone number of the tenants' former landlords. It's a must that you get not just the current landlord but those going back two or three rentals. (If you just ask for the current landlord, you might get a wonderful recommendation from a landlord who's just dying to get rid of a tenant!)

Call up the former landlords and ask them about the tenant. Explain that you are planning to rent your property to this tenant. Ask for a recommendation.

Some landlords are pleased to tell you all they know. Others are hesitant to talk for fear that anything they say may later be used against them by the tenant. (Just as in employer-employee relationships, there have been cases in which tenants have sued former landlords over bad recommendations.)

If the landlord is hesitant to volunteer information, you can ask questions that will get you the answers you want. For example:

"Would you rerent to this tenant? Why not?"
"Would you charge a higher cleaning and security deposit
    next time? Why?"
"Would you allow this tenant to have a pet?"

In nearly all cases you can quickly find out what you need to know from the former landlord. Listen carefully to what's said. Usually the former landlord has no axe to grind, unless the tenant skipped without paying rent. Then the landlord may bend your ear telling you what a turkey the tenant was.

The credit report and former landlord recommendations are the two best sources of information about your prospective tenants. Don't skip either. They are important.

My Own Experiences

Having given you the rules about credit reports and former landlords' recommendations, let me say that I've broken them as well as kept them. I've rented to tenants with horrific credit reports. And I've rented to tenants whose former landlords told horror stories about them.

Why? A lot has to do with gut feelings and the tenants' explanations. In one case I rented to a tenant who explained her bad credit was due to a boyfriend who left her with a lot of bills. It turned out to be the truth, and she was a great tenant. In another case I rented to a tenant whose former landlord said he left the place a mess with real damage done and never paid the rent on time. The tenant explained that he left it clean, paid the rent on time, but the former landlord was mad because he moved out over a dispute over painting. The former landlord had promised to repaint the insides of the house and reneged. I believed the tenant, and again, he turned out great.

As I said, it's a judgment call.

Rule 4. Don't Try to Avoid Children or Pets

This seems to fly in the face of advice that most landlords give. They say avoid renting to tenants with children whenever possible and avoid pets like the plague. Both can do damage to the property.

That certainly is true. However, besides antidiscrimination laws that prohibit the landlord from excluding children, the most reliable tenants tend to be the ones with kids. Family people tend to take care of property and pay the rent on time. If you try to avoid renting to families with kids, you may eliminate your best source of tenants. And, as noted, you could be breaking an antidiscrimination law that could put you in hot water.

Instead of not taking kids, try to rent to people who don't have more kids than the house can hold. If you rent to families with too many children, the house will show excessive wear and tear. Where allowed, try to limit the number of children in the rental agreement. (Also, be aware that small children are sometimes terrible tenants since they tend to write on the walls in crayon, which won't come off and is very difficult to paint over.)

In the case of dogs, I follow the philosophy of an old friend who at one time managed over 150 rentals. He says, "People always lie about dogs. They always say they don't have any, and then, once they move in, the dog appears. So what's the point of saying no dogs in the rental agreement? Are you going to throw out a good tenant because he or she 'acquires' a dog?

"Sometimes people come right out and say they have a dog. If I say no dogs, they say they'll get rid of the pet. I would never rent to anyone who would get rid of a pet.

"As a result, I simply say that one dog is okay. If there ends up being two, I look the other way. If there's a kennel, of course, I throw them out."

Cats and birds are something else. Cats that are not properly house trained may urinate on carpets. Cat urine is virtually impossible to get out. It may result in the need to get new padding under the carpeting, new carpets themselves, or even new flooring under the padding and the carpet! I always get a heftier cleaning deposit for a cat.

Birds can make a mess, and they can leave a particular odor in the house that is hard, but not impossible, to remove. Also, birds can sometimes screech loudly at odd times during the day or night and disturb others. I'd think twice about renting to a tenant with birds.

Rule 5. Don't Try to Get the Last Month's Rent

This must certainly fly in the face of advice that most people have received. As noted earlier, the lease in which a landlord gets first and last months' rent has been the traditional rental agreement. To now suggest that a landlord not go for it might be tantamount to criticizing mom, baseball, and apple pie.

Yet my advice is not to go for first and last months' rent on a lease. Here's why.

The traditional lease in which the tenant pays first and last months' rent grew mainly out of commercial usage. It's the sort of agreement you would use if you were renting a building to a commercial tenant. If the tenant didn't pay the rent on time, you could sue to collect the rent, and you would always be one month ahead by collecting that last month's rent up front.

With a single-family house, however, realistically you're never going to sue to collect rent from a tenant who is in the premises and who isn't paying. You're simply going to want to get that tenant out and someone better in. Suing just to collect rent is the last thing you want to do. (You'll sue for unlawful detainer—eviction—when the tenant doesn't leave and doesn't pay, in which case you might hope to recoup the lost rent later as a result of that suit.)

There's another problem with first and last months' rent. What you are mainly interested in (besides collecting rent) is that the tenant leave the property in as good shape as he or she found it. First and last months' rent doesn't address that issue—a security and cleaning deposit does. Yet if you've already collected first and last months' rent, how large a security deposit can you realistically hope to get? For example, if the rent is $2,000 a month, first and last months' rent comes to $4,000. How much more can you expect a tenant to pay for a security deposit? $1,000? $500? You reach a point at which your property requires too much cash up front for any likely tenant to afford to move in.

A better way is to forgo the last month's rent paid in advance and instead get a very large cleaning and security deposit. Today most savvy landlords are insisting on a security deposit at least equal to one month's rent if not more. If the property rents for $2,000 a month, before moving in the tenant would be required to come up with $2,000 for the first month's rent plus at least another $2,000 or $2,500 in a security deposit.

TRAP

Some states limit the size of a security and cleaning deposit. The maximum you can charge may be only one-and-a-half to two times a month's rent.

The tenant who puts up that much money has something substantial to lose if the property isn't left clean. And if the tenant doesn't pay, the deposit can always be used to compensate for lost rent. A last month's rent cannot be used as a cleaning deposit. (Check with the laws in your state to be sure that security deposits can be combined with cleaning deposits and used for either reason.)

One concern is the savvy tenant who doesn't make the last month's rent payment. When you call, the tenant says, please use the cleaning and security deposit!

You can write in the rental agreement that the cleaning and security deposit is *not* to be used as the last month's rent. You can argue until you're blue in the face. But the savvy tenant knows that it will take you more than a month to evict him or her and cost you a lot more than the security deposit, so that in the end, if they use it as the last month's rent, there's not a whole lot you can do.

Usually most tenants are not that savvy (unless they've read this book!). However, even those that are and do tell you to use the cleaning and security deposit as the last month's rent will often leave the property respectably clean. The reason is that they don't want to get you too mad. If they leave the property dirty, you could always turn around and sue them in small claims court for the lost rent and the damage they did over the amount covered by the deposit.

TRAP

Some states are now requiring landlords, even landlords of single-family residences, to keep security and cleaning deposits in a separate account and to pay the tenants interest on it. Also, you may still use a "lease" form without getting the last month's rent. Finally, most states now prohibit landlords from charging a "nonrefundable" deposit. (A deposit by its very nature is refundable.) For more information, check with a good property management firm in your state.

Rule 6. Rent for Less

It's important not to be penny wise and pound foolish when you rent. The foolish landlord tries to get top dollar for a property. The wise landlord rents for just below the market.

The reasoning is simple: To get top dollar, you have to wait for a tenant. If you rent just below the market, your property will always be full.

But some newcomers to renting may ask, aren't you losing money that way?

Consider the issue this way: You're renting a house where the market for a property such as yours is $1,000 a month. So you put your property up for $970. You'll lose $30 a month because you're renting below market. At the end of a year it will mean a loss of $360.

On the other hand, you'll rent out the property immediately. All else being equal, tenants will choose your property first over similar properties renting at $1,000. Your property will be full nearly all the time. (It's the same as when you go into the super-market and see two products of equal quality next to each other—don't you buy the one that's 5 cents less than the other even though the price difference is negligible? Tenants act the same way.)

Now consider the landlord who insists on $1,000 a month. Assuming that the market value is correct, she will get it. But it might take her a month to find a tenant. She will lose $1,000 of potential rent during that month. Is it better to lose $360 or $1,000?

But, some readers may ask, you'll keep losing money year after year. After a while the other landlord has a better deal because he is charging more.

Not at all. At the end of the year, if you have a strong tenant who wants to stay, raise your rent to the market level. If it's still

$1,000, raise it to that point. The tenant shouldn't want to move because, after all, you've just adjusted the rent to the true market value. Besides, moving is a terrible hassle, and no one wants to do it for a savings of $30 a month.

On the other hand, your competitor who started at the higher price can't raise rents because he would then be *above* the market.

What we're talking about here is the rent-up period. You want to get your property rented fast because every day it's vacant costs you money. Renting just below the market will make it far more likely that you will find a tenant quickly.

Rule 7. Charge for a Late Payment

Charging a late fee sometimes works for tenants who are always late. In any event it's a good idea to include it in every rental agreement you write.

The penalty typically takes this form: In the rental agreement you include a clause that says if that tenant does not get the rent in by a certain number of days after the due date (typically five days' grace is given), there is a penalty. The penalty is usually $50 or 5 percent of the rent, whichever is smaller.

This late-payment penalty is no more enforceable than the overall rental contract (meaning that you have to go to court to get enforcement, which you would most likely not do for $50). Nevertheless, in this modern world we are all conditioned to watch out for money penalties, and tenants do too. You'd be surprised how careful they will be to get the rent in on time to avoid the penalty.

One caution: You have to enforce the clause. If the rent is late and does not contain the $50, you may want to refuse to accept the rent until the $50 is paid. Doing this means you run the small risk of not getting any rent. On the other hand, having once paid a penalty for late rent, the tenant probably will pay on time ever after.

A version of this works well with tenants who are already in the premises, who do not have such a clause in their lease, and who begin paying later and later each month. This is the rent discount. What you do is raise the rent for this tenant. Very carefully you explain that it's been so long since you've raised the rent that your costs have gone up and so forth and, in conclusion, you feel that an increase of $50 a month is warranted to take effect immediately (or upon termination of the current lease).

However, if the tenant gets the rent in on time, there will be a $50 discount. In other words, the rent may be $1,050. However, if the rent is delivered on time, it is reduced to $1,000. You'll be surprised how many tenants will work hard to get that rent in when due.

Rule 8. Don't Delay Fixing a Problem

When you become a landlord, you also assume the duties of a "fix-it person." You are expected to take care of all the little things as well as the big things that go wrong. This includes fixing leaky toilets and plugged drains, sprinkler systems that don't turn on, and light switches that don't turn off. What's more, you're expected to fix these things *quickly!*

While you might put up with a leaky toilet for weeks, a tenant who feels he or she is paying big bucks for the property won't put up with it at all. When tenants want things fixed, they want them fixed yesterday. If you don't respond and at least make the attempt to promptly correct the situation, you could lose your tenant.

TRAP

Most states allow tenants to correct defective situations themselves and then deduct the cost from the rent. This is a definite "no-no" as far as you are concerned. The tenant might hire a plumber to fix a faucet and it would cost you $100, while you could have fixed it yourself for the cost of a 35-cent washer.

If you can't fix things yourself, get the services of a contractor who can. Rest assured there will always be something to fix, and it's important to fix it fast.

Rule 9. Keep a Lookout on Your Property

A rental property is a valuable asset. You may have hundreds of thousands of dollars invested in it. You've given it up to someone to live in for several hundreds of dollars a month. But that doesn't mean that person is going to look after that asset as you would. Therefore, check up on your property.

Don't wait until the tenant doesn't pay. Check up at least once a month, even if it's only to just drive by.

Of course, you don't want to make a pest of yourself. Your rental agreement should give you the right to inspect the inside of the house with reasonable notice. But don't always be bothering a tenant who's paying the rent and keeping the place in good shape. As noted, just driving by once in a while can be enough.

When you see those lawns starting to turn brown and the flowers in front drying up, you know you've got a problem. Stop by and check it out. It's better to find out earlier than later that your tenant lost his or her job. Maybe you can help the tenant find another job or at least another lower-cost rental.

Don't let things slip. You're the one who will get hurt in the long run.

Rule 10. Don't Let the Tenant Get Behind

What can you do when the payments are late and the penalty doesn't work?

This is another judgment call. Definitely speak to the tenant. Find out what the problem is. Maybe the tenant is waiting for a check to come in. If the late payment happens infrequently and there's a good reason, perhaps it's best to overlook it.

But what if the tenant is very late—say, one or two weeks late?

Remember, your cleaning and security deposit is typically equal to only one month's rent. If the tenant is two weeks late, he or she has already used up half the security deposit. Another two weeks and it's gone. Plus, if you have to evict, there's another month or two lost.

Most savvy landlords don't accept any late rent at all. If it's more than a day or two late, they call or check with the tenant to see what the problem is. With a good tenant, it's usually an oversight, and after that the rent's right on time. With a bad tenant, it's excuses.

If the rent's more than a week late without sufficient explanation, savvy landlords send an official notice.

TIP

Notices of late rent can take various forms. Usually it's a three- or four-day notice telling the tenant to pay or quit. The time length and form is determined by each state. It is normally the first step required in an eviction. You can pick up the preprinted form from an agent or from an attorney's office. And tenants, particularly those who are regular late payers, know it.

One such notice is usually sufficient to convince a tenant that you mean business. If the tenant still refuses to pay after two weeks, most savvy landlords begin eviction (discussed next). Note: Waiting two weeks really doesn't cost you anything since most courts won't consider an unlawful detainer action to evict until the tenant is at least two weeks late in rent and has used up the security and cleaning deposit.

The above time limits, however, are not set in stone. As with most things in renting property, it's a judgment call. On the one hand, you don't want to scare, embarrass, or anger a good tenant into leaving just because one month they happened to overlook the rental due date. On the other hand, you don't want to give a bad tenant any more time than is absolutely necessary.

As I said, there is no one set answer. You have to play each case on its own merits. For myself, however, I would never let a tenant go more than two weeks without paying the rent no matter what the situation or how good I thought the tenant was. There's just too much at stake for me to lose.

Rule 11. Evict Only as a Last Resort

Finally, you may at some time in your career as a landlord need to evict a tenant who won't pay the rent and who won't quit the premises.

TIP

Remember that self-help evictions in which you physically throw the tenants out are no longer allowed. Now you need the help of the court and possibly an eviction attorney.

Don't just call any attorney. Check around with local brokers, particularly those who handle property management. Usually one or two attorneys in town do nothing but handle evictions. Call one. This attorney undoubtedly already has set fees and knows the ropes. This attorney can get the tenant out with a minimum amount of cost and time to you.

In addition, be sure that the attorney gets a judgment against the tenant for back rent owed. Often the attorney, or his or her investigators, can follow the former tenant to a new location and a new job and garnish wages to recoup your back rent. Usually their costs and fees are not deducted from the rent owed you, but they are added to the amount collected. You may eventually get back everything you are owed! (Don't count on that happening every time, however.)

By the way, just getting the unlawful detainer judgment and eviction notice isn't the end. To finally get the bad tenant out, you will probably have to pay the sheriff. The officers will come and will literally move the tenant out. (Usually even the worst tenants will voluntarily leave once they realize that the sheriff is coming.)

When a nonpaying tenant won't quit, be prepared for a loss. Chances are you'll lose some rent, at least the rent until the tenant is evicted. You'll probably also get the place back in a mess, so there will be clean-up costs. Also note that some tenants cannot be evicted! In some states a tenant who is in the last stages of pregnancy or is seriously ill and can provide a doctor's letter that he or she cannot be moved may be allowed to stay in the property—at your expense! A tenant involved in bankruptcy may make the eviction proceedings part of the bankruptcy and postpone eviction. If you stay a landlord long enough, you'll see all kinds of problems.

The bottom line is that while all sorts of problems can happen, they rarely do. You may rent property all your life and never run into a quarter of the problems we've discussed in just this one chapter. On the other hand, you could be unlucky and get them all in the first year!

Most landlords are successful and go on to later sell their properties for hefty profits.

For more information on landlording, check my book *The Landlord's Troubleshooter*, Third Edition (Dearborn/Kaplan, 2004).

Raising Rents to Increase the Positive Cash Flow

Look for cash cows when you buy rentals, and watch out for those snapping alligators.

We're actually talking money here—positive money versus negative money (the kind that you must take out of your pocket each month just to keep your rental property going). And comparing real estate to animals just helps get the point across.

A cow is a producing property. It gets milked every day, meaning that it delivers positive cash flow to you. It puts money into your pocket.

An alligator, on the other hand, is a property with lots of negative cash flow. It requires that you take money out of your pocket to feed it.

If you've ever had a cow or an alligator, you instantly know what I'm talking about. If this is new to you, then here's an example. You've bought a house that you consider a wonderful investment. However, after you're in, you discover to your dismay that the maximum you can rent it for is $1,000 a month. However, your payments including mortgage, taxes, insurance, and maintenance and repairs are running $2,000 a month. That means that just to keep the property afloat, you have to put in a grand a month of your own money.

You can see why, in the trade, this is called an "alligator." It is, financially speaking, eating you alive.

On the other hand, let's say you buy a property and discover that you actually have positive cash flow. In our previous example, you are able to rent the property out for $2,200 a month—a $200 cash profit.

The cow provides you with milk and cream each month.

TIP

Notice that here we're talking strictly cash, not depreciation. Depreciation is a paper deduction that you take on investment real estate and that you may or may not be able to apply to your ordinary income for a tax savings.

Ideally you'll buy a cow and avoid buying an alligator. But sometimes the best laid plans can go astray and you can end up with just what you didn't want. What do you do then?

How Much, Exactly, Is My Negative Cash Flow?

For some investors, each month brings a new surprise. They know they have negative cash flow, but they've never taken the time to figure out exactly how much. They just know that at the beginning of the month when the payments are due, they always have to put in some cash from their own regular account to cover their investment property account. I've heard investors say something like, "Gee, this month I thought it would be different."

Different? How? Why? It's easy to keep track of income—it's one check (or cash) paid to you. But it's more difficult to track expenses since there are both variable as well as regular costs. However, unless you have a handle on exactly what your expenses are, you can never turn an alligator into a cow.

Separate Accounts

The first rule of managing your real estate investment property is to set up a separate account for it. Don't commingle your rental monies with your personal monies. It's too hard to keep them straight, and it can be difficult later on to explain things if the Internal Revenue Service has a few questions.

TIP

If you have multiple properties, you don't need a separate checking account for each, but you do need a separate bookkeeping account for each.

Your bookkeeping system can be quite simple. Do it in an accounts book, or, even better, use one of the many accounting programs available for your computer. (Quicken and Microsoft have excellent systems.)

Set up your system so that you have two separate pages, one for income, the other for expenses.

Income

On the income side enter the address of the property and the name of the tenant. I also write down important facts such as the amount of the security deposit, the number of renters, and the number and type of pets (and if it's a lease, when the term is up). Then each month, write down when the rent check was received: the amount (just in case it's not a full payment) and the date. This way, later on, at a glance you can tell which tenants are paying regularly right on time and which are frequently late and by how much.

Some rentals have income other than rent. For example, there can be income from rental washers and dryers, from soft drink machines, and so forth. You should have a separate heading beneath rental income for each other type of income you receive.

TIP

I always insist that rent be paid on the first of the month so there's never an issue of the date due. When you first rent up property, your tenant may come in at the middle of the month. Theoretically, the tenant only owes half a month's rent. However, if that happens, then I insist that the tenant pay one and a half month's rent the second month in order to catch up so that payments are always due on the first of the month. I set up the rent payments to be due on the first of the month because that is when most people's rent is due. When a tenant moves out, it's easier to rent up the property to a new tenant on the first of the month than on any other day of the month.

As noted, setting up your ledger for income is usually quite simple.

Expenses

To control your expenses, you need to set up a ledger page for them. This is more difficult than tracking your income because the expenditure amounts will typically vary from month to month. However, if you keep in mind that some expenses occur regularly while others only infrequently, it makes things easier.

Set up your page to first show all regular monthly payments. These typically include the following items.

Typical Recurring Monthly Expenses on a Rental

- Mortgage payment, consisting of interest and principal, and in some cases, taxes and insurance
- Water and any other utility bills

- Gardener, pool service, or any other monthly services

Next, add separate headings for infrequent expenses. Since you can usually determine what these will be, a defined heading for each is possible.

Typical Infrequent Monthly Expenses on a Rental

- Homeowners association fees (for a condo)
- Taxes, if paid annually or twice annually rather than as part of monthly mortgage payment
- Insurance, if paid annually rather than as part of monthly mortgage payment
- Maintenance, which would include the cost of the work done by subcontractors or plumbers or electricians or handymen
- Repairs, including the cost of materials
- Clean-up when a tenant moves out, to prepare for new tenant
- Advertising to find new tenant
- Special unanticipated expenses

TIP

It's important to set aside as a monthly expense any cost paid annually such as taxes or insurance. For example, if your taxes are $4,800 a year, set aside $400 a month. That way when the taxes are due, you'll have the money with which to pay them.

It should be obvious that the expense side of the journal needn't be extensive. It is, however, important that the last entry for unanticipated expenses be kept for items that occur just once. If an expense pops up more than once, create a separate heading for it.

Here's how a typical journal will look:

Income-Expense Journal for Investment Property

INCOME		EXPENSES	
DATE	AMOUNT	DATE	AMOUNT
10/1/XX	$1,500 (Rent)	10/1/XX	$1,003 (Mortgage payment)
		10/1/XX	$300 (Taxes prorated)
		10/1/XX	$47 (Insurance prorated)
		10/1/XX	$65 (Gardener)
		10/17/XX	$280 (Maintenance: Sewer cleaning)
		10/20/XX	$45 (Water)
		10/21/XX	$218 (Maintenance: Fix windows)
		10/27/XX	$517 (Repairs: Replace water heater)
			Total: $2,625

What should be clear is that this property is financially hemorrhaging: The investor had to take $1,125 out of pocket this month just to keep the property afloat.

However, a closer examination reveals that the property should actually be able to achieve a positive cash flow. If you consider just mortgage, taxes, and insurance, the total costs are only $1,350 a month. The income is over $1,500, so that's a positive situation, until maintenance and repairs are added in.

The benefit of setting up a journal in this fashion is that it immediately shows what the problem is. The investor has to work at keeping down repairs and maintenance. If he or she is successful, the income and expenses will balance out over time. If not, the property will eat the investor alive with expenses.

Can I Cut Expenses?

In the example above, it should be at least theoretically possible to cut expenses because presumably they occur only on an occasional basis. The situation would actually be much worse if the monthly negative remained the same, but instead of coming from repairs and maintenance, it came from the mortgage payment, taxes, and insurance. These are the fixed expenses that are very difficult (but not impossible) to lower.

How then can you cut expenses? The answer is that you have to be creative. Let's consider each category:

Mortgage Payments. This is a fixed expense, and the only realistic way to reduce it is to refinance to a lower interest rate or a different type of mortgage. A lower interest rate will produce a lower monthly payment. Moving from a fixed-rate mortgage to an adjustable-rate mortgage with a low initial rate could also produce a lower monthly payment, at least for the first few years. (This means that the investor will need to sell or refinance again after a few years when the adjustable's rate and monthly payments reset and go up.)

Taxes Prorated. The only way to lower this amount is to have the property's tax value reassessed. But this is unlikely to produce a reduction unless property values overall have been dropping. (Indeed, a reassessment in a hot market can actually result in an increase in taxes!)

Insurance Prorated. It might be possible to produce a marginal reduction in costs by seeking out a cheaper insurance policy.

Water. The temptation is to make the tenant pay for water (he or she pays for the other utilities) and cut this cost. That, however, might be a mistake. The result could be the tenant's cutting back on watering the landscaping, which would then die and would adversely affect the overall value of the property.

Gardener. Again, it might be a mistake to cut this because the gardener will maintain the landscaping. An alternative is for the investor-owner to spend a few days a month doing the gardening.

Maintenance. This has been a heavy expense. If you call a plumber out to fix a faucet that only needs a new washer, you may incur a $100 charge for a 35-cent part. Many investors cut these types of costs to the bare minimum by doing the work themselves.

Repairs. It could be argued that this investor was just unlucky. There was a water heater replacement. Perhaps there won't be any more repairs for the rest of the year . . . or not. If it's an older property, repairs will be a constant problem. The solution is to buy more wisely by purchasing a newer home that will likely have fewer such problems. Once purchased, however, the only alternative is to seek the cheapest repair possible. Sometimes this involves the owner-investor doing the work himself or herself. Other times it means getting three or four bids to find the least expensive.

TRAP

You can't put off maintenance and repairs in a rental the way you might be able to in your own house. You might tolerate no hot water or a leaky roof for a few days or longer. Tenants won't. They feel they are paying rent (sometimes a very high rent), and their expectations are that the premises will be habitable and at least in as good a condition as when they originally rented. It's up to you to make it so.

Special. Good news here; there's nothing unusual cropping up.

Can I Raise Rents?

I used to have an investor friend whose standard advice was, "Don't turn off the lights; increase the income." He was saying that the way to make money was not to worry about expenses, at least those that were unavoidable. The way to profit was to increase the income. In our above example, the investor could compensate for the heavy repair and maintenance expenses if he or she increased the income to, say, $2,200 or $2,300 a month.

Can you increase rents to cover your expenses? Regardless of what my friend thought, it's unlikely.

You can do some things to make the property more valuable to renters. You can make it spotless, add a gardener or a pool service, or even offer some furniture as needed.

Doing all those things might get you $100 over market, perhaps even $200, but at the same time it will cost you money to do those things.

Overall, rentals go pretty much for their market value. And that's mostly determined by the competition given their location and size. And you can't give your rental a new location or easily make it bigger.

TIP

Sometimes you can convert inside areas to your advantage. For example, a study or den might be converted to a bedroom. Going from a two-bedroom rental to a three-bedroom could increase rent by 20 percent or more. It will, however, also increase wear and tear as more people live in the property.

All of which is to say that barring a big change in the rental market upward, you're pretty much going to be stuck with the current rental income, assuming you're at market. Of course, be sure that you're charging as much as the unit warrants; don't charge less. But don't hold out hopes of charging more.

TRAP

As noted earlier, it's a mistake to charge even $50 over market. The difference could be between renting it up immediately or waiting a month or two for a tenant who will pay more. Yes, your monthly income will be higher. But it could take years to make up for the month or two of rent that you lost while you waited to find that higher-paying tenant.

Can I Deduct Losses from My Rental Income?

Some investors feel that they can easily afford to sustain a cash loss on their rental property because they'll make it up in tax savings at the end of the year. This may or may not be a reasonable assumption.

We'll go into taxes on investment rentals in Chapter 20 in more detail, and you should always consult a tax professional regarding real estate tax issues. But in brief, unless your personal income is under $100,000 a year, you won't be able to deduct all your losses on your rental property (either cash or from depreciation) each year. If your personal income is over $150,000, you may not be able to deduct any losses from rental income!

Further, there's a big misconception among those who are unfamiliar with tax deductions as to how they work. (Those of you who regularly handle rental income deductions can move on.)

If allowed, you can take the loss on your rental property as a *deduction* against your other ordinary income. You cannot take it as a *credit*. What's the difference? A deduction lowers the income on which you pay taxes. For example, if your taxable income is $50,000 and you have a rental loss of $10,000, your taxable income is reduced to $40,000.

A credit, on the other hand, is a reduction of your taxes. If you owe $12,000 in taxes and you have a $10,000 tax credit, your taxes would be reduced to $2,000.

Losses on rental property, when allowed, are a deduction, not a credit. They reduce your income and, depending on your tax bracket, can result in some tax savings. They do not directly reduce the taxes you owe, as would a credit.

TRAP

Keep in mind that what the government giveth, it also taketh away. Tax savings received each month based on depreciation usually act to lower your tax basis. This means that when it comes time to sell, you could owe more in capital gains. However, the capital gains tax rate is relatively low (compared to what it was in previous years), which means that you may still find this to be an advantage.

Getting Professional Advice

Even if you have never previously done so, when you first buy rental property, you should get a good accountant or tax attorney to look over your tax situation. Your accountant should be able to tell you quite accurately what tax savings, if any, you'll get from owning the property. If you have savings, then you can apply these against your monthly negative to reduce it.

The best way to get rid of an alligator is to never buy it in the first place. Buy a cow and you'll get plenty of milk from your property. Buy an alligator and you'll spend all your time trying to devise ways to keep it from snapping at you.

Preparing a Rental for Sale

The two best days in your life as a real estate investor are the day you buy your first property and the day you sell it.

You've bought and you've rented. It's been several years since you got the property, and prices have moved up. Now it's time to sell. What do you do?

The first step, of course, is to remove the tenant. While you can sell a property with a tenant in it, it's much harder, particularly if you want to sell to the wider market of owner-occupants.

Hopefully, the tenant's lease agreement will provide for a neat ending. The tenant simply moves out on the appointed day, and you then begin the process of selling.

Sometimes, however, it doesn't go that smoothly, and needing to get the tenants out when they would prefer not to move is the best argument I can think of for using a month-to-month rental agreement. Under the terms of such a tenancy, either you or the tenant can terminate the arrangement simply by giving 30 to 60 days' written notice. (The time depends on your state's laws.) Just tell the tenant to leave in a month or two. What could be easier?

TIP

Don't try to sell a property with a tenant in residence. Tenants don't like to show property—that's only inconvenience for them. Some will actively go out of their way to sink any possible sale in order to be able to keep renting. Get the tenant out *before* you put the property up for sale.

Of course, as noted earlier, against advice many investor-landlords prefer a long-term lease. With a lease, the sale is subject to the tenancy. If the lease has eight months left to run and you decide to sell right now, normally the tenant has the right to remain in the property for eight more months.

If you had the foresight to set up a month-to-month tenancy, removing the tenant should be fairly easy. But if you signed onto a lease, you may have to use more creative means to remove the tenant.

How Do I Break the Lease?

Depending on how the lease was written, you may have various outs. If the tenant has been late with rent or has not kept the property in good shape or has done something else to violate the terms of the lease, you could have a lease breaker.

Simply confront the tenant with the facts and point out the alternatives—either the tenant leave in a reasonable amount of time (30 days), or you'll take the tenant to court over the lease breaker. Most residential tenants will prefer to leave than to fight with an angry landlord.

TIP

If the tenant does fight, however, you will have to prove that there is, in fact, a lease breaker and that you did give the tenant an opportunity to make good and the tenant refused. That's not always such an easy row to hoe.

If there is no lease breaker, or the tenant is adamant about staying, then you may want to try to make a financial settlement. If, for example, there are eight months left on the lease, you may want to pay the tenant a few months' rent to move out immediately.

What! You may be asking yourself if you read that correctly—pay the tenant?!

Yes, pay the tenant to get back your right to occupy the property. The tenant has the right for eight months, so it will cost you something to get that right back. Of course, don't start by offering several months' rent—start by offering a month's rent and increase as necessary.

If you offer enough, almost all tenants will be eager to move. After all, they can take your money and go elsewhere and live rent free for a few months. That's an offer that's hard to pass up.

What If the Tenant Simply Refuses to Leave?

I've never had a tenant who refused to leave after being given a money inducement. However, I have heard of it happening. If that's the case, then if it's a lease, you'll simply have to wait the tenant out or try to sell the property with the tenant still inside, a tough proposition.

Of course, if you've got a month-to-month arrangement and the tenant refuses to go after proper notice, simply begin an *unlawful detainer action*. Find a good local attorney who handles evictions and let him or her go at it. The cost is usually around $1,500.

Should I Fix Up the Property?

If you don't fix up the property, you'll get a lower price and a delayed sale. Remember, there's *tenant ready* and *buyer ready*, and the two are completely different. Even if the tenant leaves the property in the exact same condition as it was when it was first rented, chances are it's going to be far from buyer ready.

Here are some of the things you'll need to consider when fixing up a rental for sale.

Fix-Up Work to Get a Rental Ready for Sale

- **Upgrade landscaping.** For the tenant perhaps a lawn and few shrubs were satisfactory. For sale, however, you'll want to dress up the look of the land. That means adding flowering plants, cultivating gardens, and making sure that the existing lawn and shrubs are full, green, and trimmed. All this is not usually expensive, but it can take time to accomplish.

- **Cleaning driveway and front walkway.** This is what the potential buyer will first see, and as we all know, first impressions (curb appeal) are important. You'll want to get out any oil and rust stains. For an asphalt driveway, that means recoating to give it a new look. For a concrete driveway with cracks, I suggest cutting out the cracks and rececmenting or adding brickwork. Yes, this latter can be expensive, but it's usually worth the cost in terms of a quicker sale for more money. Remember the quality of the front of the home sets up the buyer's anticipation of the home's quality overall.

- **Painting.** It goes without saying that every surface inside and out that is the least bit dingy or dirty, peeling, or is otherwise less than perfect should be painted. Use good paint, and be sure it's a professional quality job. This is where it shows.

- **Carpeting.** At the least have it cleaned. If it's worn or has stains that won't come out, replace it. These days you can get inexpensive carpeting that looks good (at least for a while). This will help the house immensely.

- **Resurfacing cabinets and counters.** Kitchens and baths sell the home. If the house is over 10 years old, consider a minor remodeling of these areas. Repainting or resurfacing cabinets is not that costly and makes a huge difference. Installing new countertops of tile, Formica®, stone, or Corian® brings the home up to a new level of elegance (and price). Yes, this is where it gets expensive.

- **Fix up.** Do what it takes to get any area of the house that looks bad into good shape. Remember, the house is only as good as its weakest link. A bad bedroom or a dilapidated basement or garage can ruin the image of quality that you want to portray.

How Much Should I Spend and How Much Should I Upgrade?

When you sell, you want top dollar for your home. However, you don't want to overdo it. Spend too much fixing and cleaning and you won't get your money out.

Let your guide be the neighborhood norms. Check out other homes for sale in the neighborhood. See what they look like and then compare them to yours. If they all have expensive granite countertops and yours has old, inexpensive Formica, upgrade to granite. Chances are you'll get your money back and more.

On the other hand, if all the homes have less expensive tile, then don't go for more expensive Corian. Just clean the tile you already have, or if it's in bad shape, replace it with the same material.

Can I Get a Second Opinion?

Yes, and it's a good idea to do so. Just because you're an investor in real estate, doesn't mean you're great at selling it. Get a pro to come in and take a look at the property. I'm speaking here of a good agent or two.

Agents deal with homes day in and day out. They see properties in good shape, bad shape, and every flavor in between. They can walk through a home in five minutes and tell you what all of the bad features are and what you should do to correct them.

The opinion of a good agent is invaluable . . . and easily obtained. Just say that you are thinking of selling your house, will consider the agent for a listing, but for now just want to know how well it shows. Agents will line up for the chance to tell you. (We'll have more to say about finding a good agent shortly.)

Listen to what the agent says. Think about it. It may seem a totally foreign idea to you. But it may give you a new and different perspective.

How Do I Estimate What It Will Cost to Fix Up the Property?

Simple: ask the experts.

After you've determined what needs to be done (see above), call in the pros who regularly do it. If you need carpeting, call in some carpet suppliers.

TIP If you haven't already discovered this, there are carpet wholesalers that cater to property managers and owners of investment real estate and who offer greatly reduced prices. Check with an agent who handles property management to find one of these in your area.

If you're going to have countertops and cabinets put in, call some people who do this kind of work. The same holds true for installing sinks and appliances, hardwood floors, and wall paneling.

But also consider doing it yourself or hiring a handyman to do it. While some work that involves the structure of the property or electricity, gas, or plumbing will demand a pro, much other work can be done by almost anyone who's handy.

You can save a huge amount of money by doing this yourself or hiring a helper. Just keep in mind, however, that the proof is in the pudding. You need to get a good result, a job that looks good and will help sell the property. If you or someone you hire hourly does the work and it turns out badly, it will have the opposite effect. It will just make it harder to sell.

Should I List with an Agent or Sell It Myself?

The statistics suggest that about 85 percent of all residential property (including investment) is sold by agents; only 15 percent is sold by owners. There's a reason.

Agents have the system. They have the multiple listing service (MLS), they have the buyers (who normally seek them out first), they have the knowledge, and it's what they do for a living. Quite frankly, to get a *quick* sale, you're probably best off listing your property with an agent.

Of course, agents also charge a hefty commission. If your property is in the $300,000 range and the agent charges 6 percent, that's $18,000 off the top that you'll need to spend. If you have the time, to save all or a part of the commission, you should consider trying to sell on your own.

How Do I Find a Good Agent?

To find a good agent, you have to know the characteristics of a good agent:

- **Honest.** The last thing you want is to be told one thing and discover later that it's something else.

- **Experienced.** You don't want to be the client that the agent learns on. You want someone with years of experience.
- **Local.** You want an agent who knows the market where your property is like the back of his or her hand. You shouldn't be telling the agent prices and comparables; the agent should be telling you without having to look them up.
- **Connected.** You want your agent to take advantage of the system that's in place. That means getting the message across to the hundreds of other agents that your property is a good deal. This can include talking your property up at agent meetings, caravanning agents to your house, and holding agent-only open houses.
- **Amiable.** In addition to being a financial advisor, a good agent should also be friendly and easy to talk to.
- **Assertive.** The agent must be strong enough to get your price from a buyer.

Do such agents exist? Yes, they certainly do. But you have to do some interviewing to find them. Don't expect the first agent to come across your transom to be perfect. Look for referrals from friends and associates. Ask the agent for recommendations from satisfied clients (at least three). Check with the Better Business Bureau and even the local district attorney, if you're suspicious, for any complaints. Do the same due diligence you would if you were entrusting $200,000 (or whatever your sales price will be) to a finance person. You are!

How Do I Sell It Myself?

I always advise every investor to give it a shot at selling "by owner." You won't know if you could have done it and saved all that money unless you try. But set a time limit, say, a month or two. If you haven't successfully sold it by then, bite the bullet and go with a professional.

If you're going to sell by yourself, don't give up on the idea of using agents. You can usually give a buyer's agent half a commission to handle the sale for you and bring in a buyer. Half a loaf is better than none at all. Just put "Will Cobroke" on your sign. Agents will know what you mean.

Besides cobroking, however, it's important to understand that you'll have to do all of the other work of selling yourself. If you're going to sell it yourself, you'll need the time and energy to take all of the following actions.

The Work of Selling Your Own Home

1. Fix up the property (which you'll have to do in any event).
2. Get a sign and stick it in the front yard.
3. Arrange and pay for newspaper advertising.
4. List your home on free services on the Internet (described in the next tip).
5. Hold your own "Open House." This means allowing anyone who shows up to go through your property.
6. Go to local companies and solicit the help of their transfer departments.
7. Create an advertisement to go on a public access channel of a local TV station.
8. Create flyers and put them out on your "For Sale" sign, in grocery stores, and on public bulletin boards.
9. Be home at all times to catch phone calls from potential buyers. Yes, you can use an answering machine, but buyers often won't leave their name and number . . . you need to talk to them directly (using a cell phone helps).
10. "Sell" your home over the phone when buyers call.

11. Show your property to those buyers who call. Remember, nobody but you is screening these people. And there are some criminals out there who do make it a point of checking out FSBOs for future robberies and worse.

12. When you find a buyer, negotiate directly over price and terms.

13. Handle the paperwork, which includes the following:
    - A sales agreement
    - Disclosure statements
    - Settlement documents
    - Inspection reports
    - Escrow opening and closing instructions

14. Obtain a termite clearance. (The buyer won't be able to obtain financing without it.) Arrange for any termite damage repair work.

15. Clear the title to your property by obtaining proof that any liens or encumbrances that might have been placed against the property at any time have been removed.

16. Manage the escrow accounts and terms.

17. Deal with the buyer's anxieties and problems during the closing period.

18. Let the buyer have a final walk-through.

19. Handle a buyer who wants or needs to pull out of the deal after the agreement is signed.

20. Move out of the property (which you have to do anyway).

This list is not designed to intimidate you but rather to realistically show you what's involved. Further, you can get help online from Web sites such as www.owners.com, www.fsbo.com, and www.forsaleby owner.com. They can often direct you to professionals who will handle all the details as well as set you up with the paperwork.

On the other hand, if you don't want to do the work, don't try selling it on your own. Agents usually do earn the commissions they charge.

Once I Find a Buyer, How Do I Handle Disclosures and Inspections?

Whether you sell through an agent or by yourself, you'll usually need to give the buyer disclosures on your property. And you'll need to allow the buyer the opportunity to have a professional inspection.

It's to your advantage to offer disclosures and insist on a buyer's inspection. This way, the buyers can't later easily come back and claim that some defect was hidden that would have led them to offer less or not even buy the property. You don't want those kinds of problems.

The problem with investment real estate is that because you weren't living in the property, you may not know all of its problems.

It's easy to assume that because you've been fixing everything that the tenant called about, that you know what's wrong with your rental house. But the tenant may not have called about everything. For example, the roof may regularly leak. But because it produced only a few stains on upstairs room ceilings and there was no actual water dripping, the tenant never bothered to call. You've just been assuming the roof was okay.

Or there may be serious cracks in the slab or the foundation. But because the tenant never noticed anything through the wall-to-wall carpeting and never said anything, you weren't aware of that problem either.

If you're actually living in a home day in and day out, you'll notice far more than if you just visit it once every month or so for a few minutes.

Therefore, it's to your advantage to conduct your own thorough inspection of the property after the tenant moves out and prior to sale. You don't need to hire a professional inspector (although you may want to); you can do it yourself. Spend a day or so in the property. Check for water marks on ceilings, in the attic, and in the basement. Walk all around the perimeter looking at the foundation, the siding, the paint, the roof line, the gutters, and so on. Wiggle the fence to see if it's weak. Walk the yard to check for small sink holes. In short, spend some time learning about your property.

See No Evil, Hear No Evil, Speak No Evil—Get in Trouble! The other alternative, advocated by some, is to disclose to the buyers only what you actually know without investigation, which is probably next to nothing. As a result, your disclosures are clean. How can a buyer refuse?

Yes, but what if there's something serious with a house that the buyer later says you *should* have known about?

My own feeling is that it's better to get any problems out in the open during the negotiating period after the buyer makes an acceptable offer and before the deal closes. Once the deal is closed, I want to sleep nights not worrying about someone calling to tell me he or she has discovered a problem . . . and I certainly should have known about it.

How Do I Close the Deal?

Closing the sale of a rental home is not much different from any other closing. It's mostly up to the buyer to come through with the financing. Once that's done, and any contingencies are removed, all you have to do is provide the clear title.

The only catch is that you also must provide a ready-to-go home. Presumably the tenant is out, or you've reached an agreement with the buyer who's an investor on the tenant's staying.

The home has been cleaned. The final walk-through by the buyer goes smoothly, and you're out!

Selling

16

Getting Your Price
in Any Market

*The difference between "prime" and "subprime" real estate in
any market is whether you're the seller or you're the buyer.*

I t's not hard to sell property in any market *if* (and that's
a big *if*) you observe the three key rules for selling:

Rules for Selling in Any Market

1. **Show.** Make sure it shows well.
2. **Price.** Be competitive.
3. **Exposure.** Get the word out.

Whenever the market slows down, you'll find investor-sellers
complaining bitterly about how hard it is to find buyers, how
treacherous the market is, and how they wish they were selling
stocks and bonds instead.

Nonsense!

You can sell any house in any market. But you have to observe the three key rules noted above. Miss any one of them and the property may languish for months, perhaps years. And you, the investor, will lose.

Making the Property Ready to Show

In the last chapter we went into detail on how to convert a property from rental ready to sales ready. If you're not sure what to do to make your property ready to sell, reread that chapter.

Here we'll add one more attribute of bringing a property up to show status: *staging*.

Staging is a relatively new concept in real estate sales, and it concerns tending to the details that will create a certain impression on a potential buyer when he or she sees the property. It's like polishing the silverware or making the steak sizzle. It's what makes a property's appearance stand out from all the competitors.

If you're selling a condo, single-family home, or other piece of residential property, staging makes a big difference. You might tend to pooh-pooh it, but keep in mind that most buyers have little imagination. They tend to believe only what they see. Thus, if you give them visual candy, they are going to like it.

Staging is more than cleaning and fixing up. It's making the place look desirable. Here's a list of items that you may want to use to help stage the sale of your property.

What You Can Use to Help Stage the Property

- **Furniture.** Not much, just enough to make the home look lived in. Think of model homes in new subdivisions. And if you don't have the right furniture, everything you need can usually be rented at a nominal expense. (Don't forget to add wall coverings and pictures.)

- **Flowers.** Place flowers and greenery in strategic locations inside and in front of the home; they add beauty and color. You can buy these for a small amount at most grocery stores.
- **Lighting.** Most properties have dark corners. Eliminate them with inexpensive lighting fixtures.
- **Smells.** This is an old agent's trick: Have something cooking on the stove such as mulled cider or muffins in the oven. Offer cookies to those who come by. It costs almost nothing and adds a human touch to the property.
- **Show stoppers.** Use anything else that makes the property look so good that any buyer just can't wait to get his or her hands on it.

Every property has a range of appearances from drab and run down to sparkling. Make sure that yours looks the best it can to get the quickest sale at the highest price.

Pricing to Market

Once a long time ago, I decided to invest in gold bullion. It's readily available as a contract in the commodities market. At the time gold was much in the news as its price was going up and I thought it a quick and easy way to make a few bucks. So I bought one contract.

Suffice to say, the price of any commodity, including gold, goes up *and down*, sometimes within a single day or hour. It was my misfortune that soon after I bought, the price went down and my contract lost value.

This is not fun, I told myself, and I called my broker and told him to sell. I said sell for the same price I had bought, hoping to break even.

He apologetically said that was impossible. Since I had bought, the price had fallen and I could now only sell at a loss. But, I explained, I didn't want to take a loss. Put it up for sale at my purchase price so I could break even.

He said he could put in a sell offer at the old higher price. But it wouldn't get filled unless and until the market came back. If I wanted to sell right away, I'd have to sell at market. So I sold at a loss.

Since then I have invested in gold and other commodities and made a profit (although nowhere near the profits made in real estate); however, the first incident taught me the following very important lessons.

Lessons Learned When Trying to Sell a Commodity

- It doesn't matter what you paid for it.
- It doesn't matter how much you owe on it.
- It doesn't matter how much of a gain or loss you'll incur on it.
- It doesn't matter how angry you get about it.
- You can only sell for what the market will bear.

It all comes down to competition. There are more than 10 million new and used properties of all kinds sold in the United States each year, and every one of them is in competition with every other. In an open market where buyers have full knowledge of what's out there (which is the case with real estate), nobody is going to pay more than the market price.

You want to waste a lot of time trying unsuccessfully to sell your property? Just ask *over* market.

You want to sell tomorrow? Ask *at* market.

It's just that simple—provided, of course, that you've observed the first rule noted above and you've gotten your property ready to show.

Getting to the Right Price

Earlier we talked about getting a *comparative market analysis* (CMA) to see what a property you were thinking about buying was really worth. Now go back and do the same thing for the property you're selling. (Reread the details about CMAs in Chapter 6 if you're not sure how to do it.)

Expect to come up with a short range. For example, properties similar to yours may be selling in the price range of $255,000 to $275,000. If that's the case, then the most you can expect to receive is $275,000, and that's if you wait longer. For a quicker sale, you'll need to ask the bottom of the range, $255,000.

But, you may say, just a year ago similar properties were selling for over $300,000. What about asking that much?

Doesn't matter. Remember when I wanted to sell my gold for the higher price I paid rather than the lower market price? It doesn't work. Why should a buyer pay yesterday's higher prices when today's prices are lower? Similarly when the market's moving up, why should a seller sell for yesterday's lower prices when today's prices are higher?

Forward Pricing. Keep in mind that buyers tend to *forward* price. In other words, if the market's falling, buyers tend to be wary about paying the current market price fearing that tomorrow the property may be worth even less. That produces a kind of self-fulfilling prophecy driving prices ever lower. (It also works in reverse when the market's rising.)

When you're the seller, you have to get ahead of the wave. If the market's slowing, you may have to offer below market just to entice a buyer to make a move. Of course, if the market's accelerating, it's much more satisfying—you can ask more.

Getting Enough Exposure

Finally, you have to get enough exposure.

The art of selling comes into play when you try to hook up with that buyer who wants just the property you're selling. How do you make that connection? How do you put buyer and property together?

If it were easy to do that, there wouldn't be many real estate agents out there. While the agent earns some of his or her fee from doing the documentation and closing work, he or she earns most of the fee from finding a buyer "ready, willing, and able" to make the purchase. (Indeed, according to real estate law in almost all states, an agent has earned a commission when he or she simply brings to the seller a buyer who is ready, willing, and able to purchase, *whether or not a sale is concluded.*)

When you're trying to sell your investment property, you need to bring buyer and property together. One obvious way is to get a good real estate agent. Another is to try doing it yourself. We covered both of these in detail in the previous chapter. Here we're going to talk about exposure in more general terms.

The more potential buyers who learn that your property is for sale, the better your chances of selling it whether you're doing it alone or with an agent. Therefore, as soon as it's ready to show, talk up your property.

Tell everyone you know it's for sale. Either through an agent or on your own, advertise in as many venues where buyers look as possible including newspapers, the Internet, "throwaway" housing magazines, bulletin boards, housing offices, and so on.

If you're using an agent, as most sellers do, choose your agent carefully. Pay special attention that your agent is *local*. This means he or she not only knows the local market but also all of the other local agents.

Remember, most buyers work with agents. A *local* agent can contact other agents in the area and indicate what a wonderful place you have for sale. Working the system, I've seen good agents come up with buyers within a few days of listing the house, provided of course, that it shows well and is priced right.

The Bottom Line

If you're going to be successful selling your home in any market, you've got to follow the rules. Remember, make sure your property:

- Shows well
- Is priced right
- Gets enough exposure

Do all three and you'll get your quick sale.

Ready-Made Buyers

Why go searching for a buyer when one is already living in your rental property?

Who could be a better buyer for your property than the tenant who is already living in it? Think of the advantages:

- The tenant already knows the property; you don't have to show it to him or her.
- The tenant has plenty of time to acquire the needed down payment as well as arrange for financing.
- The tenant will take extra good care of the property if he or she knows it will later become his or her own home.

Of course, not all tenants are suitable buyers. Some don't have the cash. Others don't have the income to qualify for an appropriate mortgage. And others are simply happy to rent—they don't want to buy.

All of which is to say that while a tenant can be a perfect buyer, not all tenants are. The question is how to find just the right tenant who will become the perfect buyer.

How Do I Find a Tenant-Buyer?

One method is to simply rent the property to the best available tenant. Then, a few years later when you're ready to sell, you simply ask the tenant, "Would you like to buy the home in which you're living?"

Chances are, however, you'll get a negative answer. Most tenants, I have found, would rather move to someplace else—either renting or buying another home—than buy the property in which they are living. Converting a tenant to a buyer *at the end of the rental period* can be a hard sell.

But if you sell the tenants on the idea of purchasing the property at the time you first rent to them, it's a different matter entirely. Then, during their entire rental stay, they will be seeing the property in a different light. It will be their permanent home. They are simply renting it until it's convenient to make the purchase.

In short, instead of looking for a tenant, when you want to rent out your investment property, look for a buyer who will be willing to handle a delayed purchase.

What Is a Delayed Purchase?

Today more people than ever before in history (more than 65 million) own their own homes in the United States. And many more would love to do so. People in general understand that an owned home is a great investment: it provides financial security, privacy, and most of all, profit.

However, a great many people simply can't afford to buy out-right. Rather, while their first desire is to purchase, their wallet dictates waiting.

These are the people you want as tenants—the not-quite-ready-to-buy buyers.

How do you find these people? You advertise for them!

Where Will I Find a Delayed-Purchase Buyer?

Even if you're not familiar with this approach, you've probably seen the ads for it in local newspapers. They usually read something like "Rent to Own!" or "Rent Now, Buy Later!" They sometimes will appear in the property rental section rather than in the homes for sale section, although placing them in either location works.

The idea here is that you're looking for more than a tenant. You don't want someone with a strictly rental mindset. You want some-one who is thinking ahead to ownership. When you qualify this person, you actually do two different kinds of checking up. In the first case, you look at him or her as a potential tenant. In the second case, you also qualify him or her as a purchaser.

This means that you determine whether or not the applicant can qualify for a mortgage big enough to handle your property and whether or not he or she can come up with enough cash for the down payment within the next two or three years (or however long you plan to rent before selling). A few quick calls to a loan

TIP As we've seen, financing these days has changed to the point where it is possible for buyers to get into a property with as little as nothing down. This means, how-ever, that they must be top credit risks, and, unfortunately, oftentimes tenants do not fill this ticket. Therefore, you must determine how big a down payment they will realistically need to buy your property and what the actual chances are that they can come up with the money.

broker (made with the applicant's cooperation) will usually answer the first question. The second, however, usually requires a bit of guesswork on your part.

Should I Use a Lease-Option?

A lease-option (also known in some states as a "lease with an option to buy") is a very common way to both rent and sell a property at the same time. It is used in almost all states, although a few, such as Texas, put stringent restrictions on it. Check with a good local agent to find out how your state regulates lease-options. Here's how they usually work.

The Lease

You enter into a tenancy agreement with the tenant. This is in the form of a lease. It is for a specific period of time and a total amount of rent. The time can be for a year, three years, or whatever. The form usually specifies what the tenant may and may not do to the property, includes a security and cleaning deposit, speaks to the issue of pets and the number of occupants, and so on. It's the same sort of rental agreement that you would use if you were simply involved in being a landlord.

The Option

At the same time as you lease the property, you also give the tenant an option to purchase it. In its concept, this is no different from any other option whether it involves stocks or real estate. It gives the tenants the choice to buy or not buy the property at some future date.

TIP

Note that the option favors the tenants—it's their right to buy. You are locked into selling to them *if* they choose to execute their option. Of course, since you want to sell, this is exactly what you're hoping they will do!

The Combo

The lease and the option are usually locked together in several ways. For one, you presumably would not offer the option unless the other party also agreed to rent your property. And you would not allow the applicant to rent your house unless he or she also agreed to take the option to purchase.

Further, it is common for optionees (the tenants) to pay for the privilege. They might, for example, give you $1,000 (in addition to any rent monies) exclusively for the right to get the option. Any option money you get is yours. It never has to be returned, although it is usually considered part of the purchase price when the tenants eventually buy. Separate option money, however, is not normally required for the option to be valid. You can consider the first month's rent, for example, as the option money.

TIP

My own experience is that you'll do better if the tenants put up some separate option money and they understand that it will go toward the purchase price when they buy. It doesn't have to be much; even just $500 will do. The option money works to the seller's advantage in that it cements the idea of the purchase in the minds of the tenants. By putting up that nonrefundable amount, they become locked into the concept of purchasing the home and putting that money to good use. They always remember that if they don't purchase, they lose the option money.

Rent Applied to Purchase

The real key to the lease-option, however, is that you will give a portion of each month's rent toward the down payment required to make the purchase of the property. Mention this and you will see potential tenants' ears perk right up. They will instantly see the benefit to themselves.

That's correct. You will apply a portion of each month's rent toward the eventual down payment. Be sure you understand this important angle: If the rent is $1,000, you might apply $400 toward the down payment. This means that at the end of a year, the tenants would have $4,800 in credit toward a down payment. The amount would swell to almost $15,000 by the end of the three years.

Tenants who are cash poor immediately see this as an easy way to get into ownership. If saving has been hard for them, this is as simple as falling off a log. If you're honest, something they will want to be assured of, they know that their nest egg is growing with each monthly payment. This is a far cry from paying normal rent where the tenants' money is simply lost.

The success or failure of the lease-option (as measured by whether or not the tenants eventually convert to buyers) usually hinges on how big a portion of the rent you give toward the down payment. If the amount is too small, the tenants won't value it and won't mind losing it. However, if it's big enough that the tenants can see their down payment accumulating right in front of their eyes, they will make the effort to buy rather than lose all that money.

Of course, you may be wondering about giving away a portion of the rent to the tenants. Doesn't that mean less money for you? Yes . . . and no.

To begin, remember that you're collecting the rent each month, and you can use it toward paying your investment expenses (mortgage, taxes, insurance, maintenance, and so forth). You usually don't have to separately bank the amount that eventually goes toward the down payment. You can just give that as a credit to the buyers when they purchase.

Second, you can often *charge a higher rent!*

Yes, you can charge higher-than-market rent for a lease-option. Tenant-buyers are willing to pay more because they see it as part of a purchase, not just as a tenancy. For example, let's say that the market rent of your property is $1,000. You might be able to charge $1,350 rent on a lease-option. Then, if you credit the tenants with $500 a month toward the purchase, it's only really costing you $150. (The other $350 came from the inflated rental amount.) Of course, you have access to that higher amount of rent during the entire rental period.

TRAP

Remember, the more you credit the tenant-buyers with putting money toward the down payment, the better chance of a successful sale. Make the credit too small and they may not buy.

Does a Lease-Option Have Risks?

It has one big downside. If the tenants begin to see that they won't be able to buy the property toward the end of the lease-option period, they may get resentful about paying higher-than-market rent. They could abandon the property and leave it in bad shape.

Will tenants do this?

Consider their position. If you're the tenants, you're paying higher-than-market rent. (Tenants always know what the going rental rate is—don't think you can fool them!) As a tenant, you're willing to put up with this because you know the money is going toward a down payment and toward the purchase of the property.

But what if halfway through the rental period, you begin to realize that the amount being put aside each month isn't nearly enough to cover your down payment (and, perhaps, some of the closing costs)? What if you begin to see that you won't qualify for a mortgage at the end of the agreement? What if you come to understand that you won't have enough money to make the purchase?

Then you begin getting angry about that extra rental money you're paying. You see it going into the landlord's pocket and providing no benefit whatsoever to you. You begin to see the lease-option as a device that's taking advantage of you; you'll eventually move out with nothing, and the landlord will have gotten all that extra money.

Many tenants in this position come to two realizations. The first is that they want out. So they abandon the property. This isn't bad for you in the sense that you at least get it back and can then rerent or work out another lease-option.

The other realization, unfortunately, is that they want to get even. They want something in return for all that extra money they've paid each month that now won't be going toward the purchase. And they may take their anger out on the property, not only leaving it a mess but causing serious damage.

Don't think that this can't ever happen. I have seen too many situations in which **TIP** the investors took back property from a failed lease-option and had to put thousands in to clean and repair it.

Can I Mitigate the Risks?

Of course you can. The way to reduce the risk of a failed lease-option, as noted earlier, is to increase the credit you give the tenant toward the purchase price. The more of the monthly rent that goes toward the purchase, the more likely the tenant will be able to make the eventual purchase. And, as a result, the more likely the tenant will stick it out to a successful conclusion.

Further, do a better job of qualifying the tenant at the beginning. Choose a tenant who has the ability to get the necessary financing to make the eventual purchase.

Are There Any Other Risks?

The other risks to you, the investor, are probably no more than you would face in any rental situation. The tenant could lose his or her job, be unable to make the rent payment, and leave. Or the tenants could have a divorce, or a medical problem, or even a death. Or, the market could take a big swing upward during the lease-option period and you couldn't benefit, because you were locked into an earlier price. (Some lease-options include an inflation or a market-price escalation clause to get around this. See below.)

There are no certainties when renting, and the same applies with a lease-option.

TRAP

The risks to the tenant can be more severe. The tenant risks your not being able to give a clear title when it comes time to transfer the property; that you could further encumber the property with mortgages making it worth less than the agreed-on purchase price; that you could go into debt and have liens attached to the property; and more. It is for this reason that some states will not allow you to use a lease-option unless you virtually own the property free and clear—check with an attorney in your area.

How Do I Qualify a Tenant-Buyer?

We've now come full circle back to finding the right person for the lease-option. Only now you know what you're looking for. You want someone who is basically cash poor who can make substantial rental payments. You also want someone with good credit whom you can rely upon to eventually qualify for a needed purchase mortgage. But you don't want someone with impeccable credit who can get a little- to nothing-down mortgage today and, hence, doesn't really need you.

Does this person exist? Of course. You're most likely to find your target lessee-optionee in the form of a young couple just

TIP

Be sure to ask your would-be tenant-buyer to get a mortgage preapproval and to show it to you. This usually is available for just the cost of a credit check, typically under $50. It will show how big a mortgage and monthly loan payment the potential tenant-buyer can currently afford. If it turns out that he or she is nowhere near being able to qualify for a loan big enough to buy your property, you may want to pass on that particular applicant.

starting out. (Usually older people have accumulated some savings.) Your best bet is to seek (advertise) for them in areas where there are lots of apartment rentals.

Are There Additional Advantages to Using a Lease-Option?

We've already discussed some of the plusses, the biggest of which is that you lock in a buyer (or at least try to) as soon as you acquire the property. That means you don't have to go hunting later on. Here are some additional advantages.

Additional Advantages of a Lease-Option

- If you handle the work yourself, you won't need to hire an agent and pay a commission a few years later when it comes time to sell. This can be a substantial savings. (Note, however, that if you hire an agent to find a lessee-optionee for you, the agent will usually charge a rental fee and an eventual commission.)
- You retain control. With a lease-option, the title to the property doesn't pass from you to the other party until the sale is actually concluded. Therefore, there is little chance for you to lose your money as might be the case if you sold and retained a second mortgage in lieu of a full down payment, and then the buyers didn't make the payments.

Are There Additional Disadvantages to Using a Lease-Option?

We have already talked about the tenant possibly getting mad and leaving the place a mess if he or she cannot eventually complete the purchase of the property. However, the greatest disadvantage we haven't discussed yet, which is that you're locked into a sale.

Remember, the option is with the buyer, not with you. The lessee-optionee has the choice of going through with the purchase or not. *You don't have the choice of not selling.* If the tenants decide to buy, you *must* sell to them under the terms of the option.

What If I Change My Mind?

What if you give a three-year lease-option and at the end of that time you discover the value of the property has nearly doubled (as happened in recent years)? Now you decide you'd rather hang onto the property than sell.

If the tenants want to exercise their option to buy, you could try negotiating with them. You could even pay them money to not execute their option! However, if they were determined to purchase, they could demand that you sell and, if necessary, take you to court to force their rights.

There is another solution here. A savvy investor will put an *inflation clause* (noted earlier) into the lease-option. The clause says that the price will go up depending on a certain index. It could be keyed to overall inflation, or it could be keyed to the price increase in housing in your area as measured by some independent index (which would have been a winner for sellers in most areas in recent years).

In this way you're protected from having to sell at a price significantly lower than market.

TRAP

Savvy tenant-buyers who will go along with some sort of an inflation clause often will also demand that it be reciprocal. In other words, yes, they'll pay more if the price of the home increases. But, on other side of the coin, they'll want to pay less if the price goes down! In others words, the price will be linked to the housing market up . . . or down.

How to Flip Properties

When you are buying to live in it, you're allowed to fall in love with the property. When you are buying to make an investment, you're not.

Flipping properties usually means selling them shortly after buying. The big problem with doing that, of course, is the cost of the transactions, typically 10 percent of the purchase price when you include the selling agent's commission.

Often a better approach is to never take title—to never actually complete the purchase. Rather, you gain control of the property and then sell it out of escrow. That's what we'll examine in this chapter.

Flipping a Property Using a Real Estate Option to Buy

As we saw in the last chapter real estate options are, in reality, not much different from stock options. For the buyer they are an opportunity but not a requirement to purchase for a set price by some future date. For the seller they are a commitment to sell for a set price by a set date.

How an Option Works

1. You locate the property and make an option offer.
2. If the seller accepts, you give the seller some option money. The seller gives you the option to buy the property at a fixed price for a certain amount of time.
3. You later exercise your option by buying the property, or in our case, by selling your option to a rebuyer for a profit.

Note that in an option, you the buyer are *not* committed to purchase. Whether or not to purchase is at your discretion. The seller, however, is committed to sell. He or see must go through with the transaction *if* you execute your option. (Of course, whether you buy or not, you don't get your option money back.)

How an Option Benefits the Seller

As noted, in order to get an option, you pay the seller some money. It can be any amount, but it has to be enough to persuade him or her to give you an option. A typical amount might be between $500 and $5,000, depending on the value of the property.

The term of the option is likewise negotiable. Usually they run from 30 days to six months, but they can be for almost any length.

Once you find a buyer, which we'll call a "rebuyer," you sell that person the property. Escrow is opened, and as part of the process, your option is exercised. The rebuyer purchases the property, which you technically get from the seller by exercising your option. As a practical matter, the rebuyer gets a new mortgage and puts up a down payment, the seller gets his or her price as defined by the option agreement, and you get the difference.

Plusses of the Option

- You've tied up the property at a fixed price.
- You don't have to qualify for or obtain a mortgage. You also don't have to come up with a down payment.
- You have time to find a rebuyer, often as long as six months or more.
- You don't own the property, so you're not responsible for mortgage payments, taxes, insurance, maintenance, or repairs.
- You've got a relatively small amount of cash tied up.

Minuses of the Option

- You have to put up some money. (Obviously, as little as possible.) The seller gets this money and keeps it. Depending on how the option is written, it may be deducted from the sales price to you when and if you exercise your option.
- If you don't exercise your option before it expires, you lose your option money (the amount you put up).
- If property values go down during the option period, you'll have trouble finding a rebuyer.
- It takes time, and the seller may want a quick, clean sale—hence, it may be hard to convince a seller to go along with an option.

I've given and taken options on real estate. They can work for both buyers and sellers. For the buyer, an option offers some obvious advantages such as tying up the property for a small amount of money and giving the buyer time to locate a rebuyer and conclude a sale. For a seller, an option provides some immediate income (the option money) and (hopefully) a reliable sale.

Situations Not Favorable for Using Options

The biggest problem with options, as far as I'm concerned, is that usually sellers want a quick, rather than a delayed, sale. They may be planning on using the money from the sale of their property to buy another. They may be facing foreclosure or other financial problems. There could be a divorce or a death in the family. In all such cases, they may need to get cash now. Your offer of an option may be appealing, but it won't cut the mustard if they need to be out of the property within a month or two (which, indeed, may be the compelling reason they are willing to sell for a low price).

If you can't get an option, another way to tie up the property without buying it is to use an assignment of purchase.

Flipping a Property Using an Assignment

Here you make an offer to purchase, usually for cash. However, when you make your offer, you state that the buyer is your name "or assigns" (or whatever language is appropriate for your state). What this means is that either you can buy the property or anyone else you assign the contract to can buy the property.

The problem here is that savvy sellers often won't agree to an assignment in a sales contract. The reason is that they don't know who will eventually purchase the property. They are afraid that you might not be able to get a needed mortgage and want a back door out, or that you're planning to sell your contract to someone else (which is, in fact, the case) and that person may not qualify for a needed mortgage. In order to calm the seller's fears that the sale may fall apart, you may need to put up a bigger deposit or avoid putting many escape clauses into the contract, which can increase your risks.

Unlike the option, the assignment runs for as long as a normal closing period, typically 30 to 45 days. That means that you've got to find a rebuyer and conclude your other end of the deal very quickly. This, of course, adds to the risk.

Hopefully you'll have done your homework and have a rebuyer waiting in the wings. You now sign a separate agreement for the property with the rebuyer, but of course your resale is for a higher price than your purchase. When the deal is ready to close, the rebuyer actually takes the title to the property.

Again, you never actually make the purchase. The transaction is basically handled in escrow. At the end of the deal, you get your money out, typically in cash.

Plusses of an Assignment

- There is little cash involved. The only money you have to put up is the original deposit that you pay the seller when you make your offer to purchase, and you get this back from your rebuyer.
- It's a quick deal. You can expect to get your profit out within 30 to 45 days.
- You don't have to qualify for or obtain a mortgage.
- You don't own the property, so you're not responsible for mortgage payments, taxes, insurance, maintenance, or repairs.

Minuses of an Assignment

- You actually do commit to purchasing the property. To protect yourself from having to complete the purchase in case you can't find a rebuyer (or your rebuyer falls through), you'll want lots of escape clauses. But escape clauses weaken your offer and lessen your chances of getting it accepted. So to make the deal, you may have to take a big risk by not including escape clauses.
- If not handled properly, you can make the seller seriously mad at you.

- The seller may not be able to complete the sale for any number of reasons, so you'll again need lots of escape clauses to protect yourself from the rebuyer in case you can't close. Again, such clauses weaken your sales agreement.

Escape Clauses in Assignments

As noted above, you need to include lots of escape clauses in the deal in case you can't find a rebuyer in the short amount of time that you have, or in case that rebuyer, for some reason, can't complete the purchase.

Escape clause? What's that?

It's a very commonly used device in most real estate sales transactions. It's a clause that says the sale/purchase is "subject to" or "contingent upon" anything. If that anything happens, you may be able to gracefully (without financial harm) back out of the deal. In modern transactions, there are three widely accepted escape clauses that most sellers will agree to without blinking (and that won't weaken the chances that the transaction will go through):

Common Escape Clauses That Can Let You Get Out of the Deal

1. **Financing contingency.** You have written into the contract that the deal is contingent upon your getting financing. No financing, no deal, and you're out without penalty. This usually runs for 30 days, but you must reasonably look for financing.

2. **Disclosure contingency.** You must approve the seller's disclosures. If you don't approve them, there's no deal. But the time limit here is very short. In California, for example, it's statutorily three days.

3. **Professional inspection.** You must approve a professional inspector's report. Don't approve it and there's no deal. Usually you have 14 days to get the report and then either approve or disapprove it.

Note that there are other common escape clauses, such as one making the deal contingent upon your first selling an existing house, but these usually don't apply to an investor.

The problem with these contingencies is that they probably don't offer you enough protection if you're using an assignment. For example, in order to get the deal at a cut-rate price, you may have to offer the seller cash. In a cash sale, you don't have the protection of a financing contingency.

You might rely on the disclosure and professional inspection contingencies, but those usually run out after 14 days at maximum. At that time you either agree to move forward without their protection or back out of the deal. If you agree to move forward and something adverse happens (your rebuyer peters out), you're stuck with the house!

Adding Other Contingencies

As a result, most investors who are flipping by using an assignment want to add other contingencies. This is easy to do, but it is not easy to get them accepted by the seller.

You can make the sale contingent on anything: your uncle dying and giving you an inheritance, your great aunt coming from Australia to approve the deal, sun spots, or anything at all. However, any contingency you add that's not reasonable (that is, any contingency other than the three common ones listed above) is likely to be considered frivolous by the seller and a reason not to sell to you. Thus, the more escape clauses you include, the less likely you are to get the seller to sign. And the fewer escape clauses you include, the greater your risk that you'll actually have to buy the home yourself in case you can't get a rebuyer to close the deal.

Some readers, I'm sure, are asking, why are all these cautions necessary for an assignment?

The reason is that an assigned purchase agreement tends to be rather iffy. There's a lot that can go astray between the time it is signed and the time it is actually concluded as a final sale between the seller and the rebuyer. If the sale can't be concluded, the seller is, of course, likely to get angry. And you want some good cover when that happens.

The Need for Full Disclosure

There's an inherent problem in using an assignment to flip a property. Unfortunately, I've yet to see midnight gurus (those who promote it on late-night television and elsewhere) explain this.

Almost all sellers want to know who's buying their property. (This is even the case with banks when dealing with REOs [foreclosures]; a bank will almost always insist on knowing exactly whom they're dealing with.) When you assign the purchase agreement, you break that bond. Most sellers, nevertheless, are willing to go along provided that the deal concludes in a reasonable fashion. After all, they're still getting a sale out of it.

However, when they discover that you're reselling the property at a substantial profit, sellers might become very unhappy. After all, they conclude, what are you adding to the deal? They feel that your profit should rightly go into their pocket.

Don't expect sellers to recognize the fact that for whatever reason, they couldn't get full market price for the property. (If they could've, they would've.) What you're bringing to the transaction is your marketing expertise.

As a result, you could have an angry seller on your hands who at the least refuses to sign off on the deal unless he or she gets more money, or at worst, wants to take you to court. Thus, to oil the waters, many investors who flip in this manner *just don't tell the sellers*. They wrongly believe that what the sellers don't know won't hurt them.

Therein lies the rub. There isn't anything illegal or even unethical in flipping property *as long as all parties involved are made aware of what's happening*. However, when one party doesn't know what's going on, there are all kinds of opportunities for things to go wrong.

If they're being frank, many investors will tell you that flipping works best in secret. If the seller doesn't realize you're making a $100,000 profit on the sale, he or she isn't likely to complain. But in the same breath those investors will also tell you to bite the bullet and let the seller know because it will save you all sorts of trouble later on.

TIP

Make all your disclosures in writing, and get signatures from all parties. That way in case someone should later have an attack of memory loss, you'll be able to produce written documentation of your disclosures.

Remember, it shouldn't make any difference what you do with property after you and the seller agree on price. If you can flip it to another buyer for a better price, so be it. Just be sure the seller knows and agrees . . . in writing.

Handling the Rebuyer

Will the rebuyer get mad at me? Probably not if you handle it wisely by letting the rebuyer know what you're paying for the property (and getting confirmation on a signed statement from the rebuyer). On the other hand, if you conceal the information, the rebuyer may discover it later on and think you were trying to pull a fast one . . . and go after you.

In fact, as long as you're selling *at market*, most rebuyers won't care in the least that you're flipping or how much you're making

232 BUY, RENT, AND SELL

on the deal. As long as they're assured they aren't paying too much, chances are they'll be happy.

Using a Hidden Double Escrow: The Wrong Way to Flip a Property

A *hidden double escrow* is designed to deceive a buyer and a seller. It's a situation in which there are two escrows on the same property held simultaneously. In one you are the buyer and in the other you are the seller. They close simultaneously—you buy the property from the seller in one and simultaneously sell it to the rebuyer in the other. In a hidden double escrow, only you know what's going on. The seller deals only with you in one escrow and the rebuyer deals only with you in the other. They never deal with each other and hence, don't have direct knowledge of the total deal. The true facts, thus, are concealed—a recipe for trouble.

It is most certainly illegal for a real estate agent to conduct a double escrow and receive an undisclosed profit from a property he or she is listing. It may be not be illegal, but it is certainly unethical for an investor to do the same thing. The simple, sure way to avoid problems is to avoid putting a property into a hidden-double-escrow situation.

The Right Way to Flip a Property

The right way to handle a flip is to be sure that all parties know what you're doing (and, as noted, you have put it in writing). Quite often when the seller and rebuyer learn of what's happening, they'll admire you for it. After all, remember that you're providing a sale for a seller who wants to get out. And you're providing a home for a rebuyer who wants to get in. Why shouldn't you be entitled to a profit for that? It's a win-win-win situation.

Mortgage, Appraisal, and Rebuyer Manipulation

What has given flipping a bad name more than anything else over the past few years are unscrupulous investors who have manipulated mortgages, appraisals, and rebuyers. Rather than do the real work of the transaction—namely, finding properties that are selling below market—they have purchased properties at actual market and then, through manipulation, sold them for above market to unwary rebuyers. This has been done in alleged collusion with lenders who have apparently secured higher appraisals than were warranted and have made bigger loans than were justified. Often these properties were sold to poorer minority rebuyers who really didn't understand about market value or how high their monthly payments would be. Subsequently, when these rebuyers couldn't make stiff payments, the houses were lost to foreclosure.

That's where the real trouble started for these unscrupulous flippers. Almost all home mortgages are one way or another insured or guaranteed through the government or a government-related agency (FHA, VA, Fannie Mae, Freddie Mac, and so forth). When the government began taking these properties back, it found out what was happening and launched criminal investigations into the flippers.

This is not something you ever want to have happen to you. Always do the right thing: Find undervalued properties; there are plenty of them out there to go around. Then let everyone know what's happening in the deal, and get legitimate loans and appraisals. You'll do the seller, the rebuyer, the government, and especially yourself a big favor.

CHAPTER 19

Converting Equity to Cash

It's not what your eye sees in real estate that counts. It's what your mind visualizes.

Few real estate investors want only one property. We've all played the game of Monopoly, and we know that fortunes are made by buying more and more property. The trick, of course, is finding a way to parlay that first rental into a second and then a third and so on.

Of course, once you've owned a property for a while, chances are you've got some equity in it. Unless the market's actually falling, the combination of equity return on your mortgage and price inflation should be building your treasure chest all the time. So it's not that you're broke—it's that your wealth is on paper. How do you convert that paper equity to cash?

Refinancing to Buy

The obvious solution to getting your cash out is to refinance your existing property. If it's a rental, almost any lender will quickly (assuming you have a decent credit score) give you 80 percent of the property's value. Some lenders will go to 90 percent, and if they don't, you can almost always get a 10 percent second mortgage.

Problems arise when you want to pull money out in excess of your original financing—when you want to cash out. For example, you may owe $160,000 on a property that has a value of $200,000, meaning you have an equity of $40,000—a nice tidy sum that could help you purchase one more additional property.

However, as soon as you approach a lender, you're likely to learn that while an 80 or even 90 percent loan plus closing costs is readily available, as soon as you want to take cash out, you're blocked. The lender is more than happy to let you refinance to a different type of mortgage or a lower interest rate *as long as you don't cash out*. As soon as you want to pull out your equity, the lender balks.

The lender's reasoning here is that by pulling your cash out, you're weakening the lender's position in the property. Not only is it concerned because you'll end up with a lower equity position but it also worries that because the property is a rental, you'll take that cash and buy another rental (which, of course, is exactly your plan!). However, now with two rentals the lender worries you might get in over your head and, if you have a spell of vacancies, end up losing a property—something it does not want to have happen.

Of course, all of this is really none of the lender's business. If you qualify for the mortgages at a higher loan-to-value (LTV) ratio, it shouldn't make any difference what you do with the money you pull out. Nevertheless, it often presents difficulty.

Solving the Problem of Cashing Out When Refinancing

Here are two solutions.

The first, as noted earlier, is to get two mortgages. You can keep the existing first you have on the property and get a new second. Or you can get a new first and second whose combined LTV will be 90 percent or higher. Typically when you get a *second* mortgage on investment property, the lender isn't nearly as concerned about whether or not you're pulling cash out. The second typically has a higher interest rate than the first, and that helps make up for any greater perceived risk on the lender's part.

The second alternative is the one that I like better. You have to live somewhere. Presumably you own the house you live in. (If not, go out and buy a house to live in immediately. The tax and financing advantages are terrific!)

So instead of refinancing the rental, refinance your personal residence.

Lenders will normally give you 80 to 90 percent of the LTV on a personal residence, and they won't balk at letting you take cash out. The reason they're so generous is simply because you're an owner-occupant.

TIP It's a good idea to refinance well in advance of your next purchase (at least six months). This will help to keep your credit from being strained.

Further, you may be able to deduct the interest on your tax return of up to $100,000 when you refinance your personal residence, over and above your original financed purchase, even if you spend that money on buying an investment property.

TRAP

The tax rules for taking money out of your personal residence are quite complex and are more limited than most people think. Generally speaking, if the money is to construct or remodel the residence, you may be able to take out more than the $100,000 noted above (up to a total encumbrance of $1 million). There is an exception for using the money for educational purposes. Be sure you check with your accountant before refinancing to be sure what the tax consequences for you will be.

An even better approach might be to refinance your personal residence, and then after a period of time, move out and convert it to a rental. In this fashion you've both gotten your cash out and you've acquired a new rental property.

Further, when you buy your next home, you can plan to move into it and make it a personal residence. As an owner-occupant, you are entitled to the best financing on earth—as little as nothing down at the lowest possible interest rate, providing that you have the appropriate credit score.

By buying and converting personal residences, refinancing to get the equity out, and doing it again and again, you can acquire many properties over time. And do it using much better financing than you would be able to obtain if you were buying properties as strictly rentals.

Handling Two Monthly Payments

When you convert your equity to cash and then buy a second property, you'll then have to make the mortgage payment both on your old home, now converted to a rental, and on the new home that you're buying. That's two payments instead of one. It's only sensible to worry about whether your income will stretch that far.

Of course, this is always the dilemma of investors in real estate. If you went out and bought a rental property, you'd also have two payments (the rental plus your own home).

Keep in mind, however, that you now have rental income. Income, after all, is the whole purpose of renting out real estate. And that rental income, if you selected the property wisely, should be enough cover at least one of your payments.

For example, if you refinanced your old home, the payments would be higher. But, hopefully, the rental income would cover most of them. Thus, you really don't have two mortgage payments to make but only one and perhaps a little extra to cover any negative cash flow.

TIP

If you leave some of your equity in your old property, you may have a low enough existing mortgage that the rental income will be higher than your monthly payments. This can help offset high payments elsewhere.

Of course, there is always the matter of risk. Your rental property (old home) could be vacant for a while before you find a suitable tenant. Or you could be unlucky and get a bad tenant who needs to be evicted, and you could lose some rental income there.

Those are a few of the risks of investing in real estate. And they're good reasons to hold some money back in reserve. However, as with all investments, you must measure the rewards. Is it worthwhile to assume the risk to get the profits available? If your answer is yes, then you may want to move forward with your conversion.

The Tax Consequences of Converting Equity to Cash

Note: The following discussion is not designed to give tax advice but simply to give an overview of a few real estate tax rules. You should not rely on it; always consult with a professional if you desire tax advice.

There shouldn't be an immediate tax consequence of refinancing. After all, you're not selling a property. You're just renting it out and/or refinancing. Thus there's no capital gain (or loss) that would trigger a tax.

However, when you file your next tax returns, your deductions for mortgage interest may be higher if you have a bigger refinancing. (See the discussion above on the allowable interest deduction on a personal residence.)

Nevertheless, one benefit that you will lose when you convert a personal residence to a rental is the ability to exclude gain on the sale of your home. Under current tax rules, an individual who sells a *principal residence* can exclude up to $250,000 of the capital gain on the sale (up to $500,000 for a married couple filing jointly). While there are other conditions that must be met, including a two-out-of-five-years residence requirement—or five-out-of-five if you previously did a 1031 tax-deferred exchange on the property— the part of the rule we're concerned with here is that the property must be your *main home*. It can't be both your main home *and* a rental property. It's either one or the other. And if it's a rental property, you lose the exclusion benefit.

TIP

If you have a multiple-family building (such as a duplex, triplex, or small apartment building), you may be able to live in one unit and rent the others out. When that's the case, the portion in which you live may have the exclusion available while the portion rented out may not.

The Two-out-of-Five-Years Rule

As noted, the residency requirement is two out of the previous five years to get the exclusion on the sale of a personal residence. However, it can be any two of the five years. That presents some interesting possibilities. For example, you could live in your existing home for two years and then rent it out for the next three. When you sell, presumably, you could still qualify for the exclusion because you had previously lived in it for two years within the five-year time frame.

Or you could have lived in it for only one year. Then you could rent it out for three years and move back in for one year, at which time you'd again qualify for the exclusion.

Thus, converting your home to a rental does not necessarily, or at least not immediately, disqualify you from receiving the benefits of the exclusion.

Furthermore, you can be building up time toward the two years in your new home. If you play the timing right, you could theoretically get the benefit of the exclusion on both properties, but only once each two years. (Be sure to see your accountant before attempting this.)

Tax-Deferred Exchanges

A Section 1031 tax-deferred exchange is often a good way of avoiding the immediate payment of tax on the gain from the sale of a rental. Instead of selling, you trade for another property of "like kind." If done properly, the gain on the one property is transferred to the next. We'll have more to say about tax-deferred exchanges in Chapter 20.

The Refinancing Process

If you intend to cash out your equity by refinancing, your first move should be to get yourself preapproved by a lender. This will let you know the maximum mortgage and monthly payment you can get.

Obtaining Preapproval for a Mortgage

Once you know the maximum mortgage and monthly payment you've been approved for, you can proceed to make a decision regarding the equity in your property. For example, if you can qualify for a big enough loan-to-value ratio, you may want to leave the equity in your existing property in place and simply buy the new home outright. This sometimes has the added benefit of giving you a lower payment on the old property, thus making it easier to cover your expenses with your rental income. (Your property then becomes a cash cow rather than a snapping alligator—see Chapter 12.)

On the other hand, if you can't get a big enough LTV ratio on a new property, you may want to refinance your old home to get your cash out, as described above. And then, after an appropriate period of time, you will want to proceed with the purchase of a new home.

Finding Your New Property

Are you going to be buying a rental outright? Or are you going to convert your existing home to a rental and buy a new personal residence?

Decide. Either way, be sure you look for the new home as if it's going to be an investment instead of looking for a home just to live in. Remember, eventually you'll probably do it again—convert that new home you live in to a rental and so on and so on. You want a property that will make a good rental. (See Chapter 12.)

TIP

Remember, you will eventually want to rent and resell any property that you buy. Therefore, it makes sense to buy with an eye toward a future tenant and buyer.

Making the Purchase

If your goal is to get cash out of your old property and if you've done it, the next purchase should be straightforward: cash down (if any) to a new loan. There's no need to make the purchase contingent on the sale of your old home (which would weaken the offer) because you're not selling your old home.

Making the Conversion

As soon as the purchase of your new home goes through and you move in, you'll want to rent out your old home. You can try to rent out your old home even before you leave. Put an ad in the newspaper and see what happens. But be prepared to have prospective tenants bothering you day and night to see the property. (It's just as bad as having to always have the place fixed up and ready to show to prospective buyers!)

Whether or not it's already rented, however, once you move out, be prepared to fix up the old house. Even though it may look clean while you're living in it, at minimum you should do the following to make it tenant ready:

- Clean the carpets.
- Paint any rooms that have scratches or marks on the walls.
- Have the kitchen and bathrooms professionally cleaned.
- Be sure all the appliances are working.
- Get all your stuff out!

Perhaps the biggest mistake that those converting old homes to rentals make is to leave some of their old stuff in the rental home. After all, when you move, you tend to get overwhelmed by the amount of stuff you've accumulated. Wouldn't it be simple to just leave a lot of it at the old place?

That won't work. Tenants expect to use the entire home, including garage and storage areas. You'll have to get all of your things out *before* the tenant can move in.

The Bottom Line

In this chapter we've looked at the advantages of refinancing to get your equity cashed out. We've also considered an investment plan that involves renting out your existing home and buying a new home for you to live in . . . and then doing it again, and again.

This is called *serial investing,* and it's done on a regular basis by probably more than a million people in the United States. To my way of thinking, it's one of the easiest ways to get rich over time in real estate.

Tax Advantages for the Real Estate Investor

The only two things in life you can't escape are death and taxes. But while there's no holding off the grim reaper, sometimes you can keep the tax collector at bay.

Special Note: The author is not engaged in providing tax advice. The following is a brief overview of some of the tax rules affecting real estate investing. These rules change with new tax bills passed by the government, IRS rulings, and precedent-setting tax cases. You should not rely on this information. For tax advice on your property, consult with a tax professional.

The first thing an owner of real estate usually learns about taxes is how to depreciate his or her property. *Depreciating* means taking a certain percentage of its *cost* (we'll talk more about this later) each year as a reduction in the property value.

Almost all business assets can be depreciated. Cars, for example, are often depreciated over a lifespan of five years. In a straight-line method, you might take 20 percent a year of the cost as a loss of value.

Residential real estate is depreciated over 27.5 years. Again, using a straight-line method, you would take 1/27.5 of the cost each year as a loss in value.

Of course, as we all know, the value of property typically goes up, not down. So how can you take a loss on an asset that's increasing in value? A helpful way to understand this is to think of it is as a *paper loss*. All assets deteriorate over time. Even a house will eventually fall away to dust. So instead of simply waiting until the end of its useful lifespan (arbitrarily decided by the government), you take a portion of the loss in value each year.

The time span of 27.5 years is specified by the government, and it is quite **TIP** arbitrary. In the past much shorter time spans have been allowed.

But, you may reasonably wonder, while the house will eventually deteriorate, the land never will. How do you depreciate land costs?

The answer is, you can't. You can depreciate only the building, not the land. The only exceptions would be if the land itself had an asset that was depletable, such as gas and oil, and presumably that's not the case here.

Is Depreciation an Expense?

Yes, it is. It's an expense much as you would have for other expenses when you own rental property. For example, here's a list of some expenses you might expect to incur:

Typical Rental Property Expenses

- Mortgage interest
- Taxes
- Insurance

- Water service
- Garbage services
- Maintenance and repairs
- Fix-up
- Advertising
- Pool and gardener services
- Depreciation

TIP

Save all your receipts! Unlike owning a principal residence where the only deductions are typically property taxes and mortgage interest, with a rental property almost every legitimate expense is deductible. You may be able to deduct a phone, auto, and even business cards! Check with your accountant.

When you add up all of the above expenses, you have the total expenses for your property over a month. Add all the monthlies together and that's how much it costs you over a year.

Now subtract your total annual expenses from your total annual income, and that's your profit or loss.

Does Depreciation Contribute to Loss?

It certainly does. As soon as you begin to look at properties out there in the real world, you'll come to realize that finding one for which the income comes close to paying for all of the actual cash expenses is rare. When you add the paper loss of depreciation to your cash expenses, you almost always find that there's a loss.

Typical Income and Expenses on a Rental House	
Total annual income:	$14,440 ($1,200 monthly)
Total annual cash expenses:	- $14,000
Positive cash flow:	$440
Annual depreciation:	- $7,500
Annual loss:	$7,060

Once depreciation is added in, you can almost always be assured that the property will show a loss, at least on paper. In our earlier example, a good property that actually shows a positive cash flow (more money coming in than cash expenses going out) turns into a big loser as soon as depreciation is added.

Remember, that the loss from depreciation is not an out-of-pocket expense. It's simply an accounting loss—that is, it shows up only on paper.

In the dim past, depreciation was a tax dodge that was used by the wealthy to reduce their sizable incomes. They would own multiple properties and take a depreciation loss (which occurred only on paper) and deduct it from their ordinary income. That reduced their ordinary income, which, of course, reduced the amount of taxes they would owe on that income. In some cases people with millions of dollars in actual income would end up owing nothing, all due to depreciation!

That tax shelter was eliminated for the wealthy by the Tax Reform Act of 1986. Now it is available only if your income is less than $150,000. We'll have more to say about this shortly.

Using Depreciation to Reduce the Tax Basis of the Property

Let's go back to when we were earlier saying that depreciation reduced the "cost" of the building by a certain amount each year. While the cost is the most common method of establishing a tax basis, it's not the only consideration.

For tax purposes there is a *basis* to each asset. That is the amount used for making tax calculations such as depreciation or when you sell for capital gain.

The basis, as we said, for most assets is their cost. However, that basis can vary. For example, there are substantial transaction fees when you buy a property. Most of these are added to the basis.

Or you may build an addition. This is also added to the basis.

On the other hand, the basis may be reduced. Depreciation reduces the basis of the property. Here's how it works:

Change in Basis Due to Depreciation	
Original basis (cost):	$200,000
Add a room:	+ $30,000
Adjusted basis:	$230,000
Depreciation ($7,000 annually for 10 years):	- $70,000
New adjusted basis:	$160,000

Notice that although the property began with a basis of $200,000, which was its cost, that basis went up when a room was added and, more importantly here, it went down when depreciation was calculated.

The Importance of the Tax Basis

Understanding how the basis is established is important because the basis (and the sales price) determines the capital gains and therefore the capital gains tax you'll have to pay when you sell.

Your capital gain on the property is the difference between the adjusted tax basis and the sales price.

Calculating the Capital Gain	
Sales price (adjusted for costs of sale such as commission):	$300,000
Adjusted tax basis:	- $160,000
Capital gain (on which tax is due):	$140,000

Thus, to go through our example, you buy the property for $200,000, add a room for $30,000, which raises your basis, and then you depreciate it for $70,000, which lowers the basis. When you sell, both the raising and lowering of the tax basis affects how big a capital gain you have.

An investor needs to keep his or her eye on the donut and not the hole. What's important here is to see that depreciation lowers the basis, which means that upon sale, there will be more capital gains (and resulting taxes).

All of which is to say that while depreciating real estate can produce a tax write-off, as noted earlier, when you sell, that tax loss can come back to haunt you as a capital gain.

How the Capital Gain Used to Be Calculated

In decades past when anyone regardless of income could write off losses on real estate, what they were actually doing was converting their ordinary income to capital gain. Instead of paying high ordinary income taxes, they converted that income to a capital gain and paid lower capital gains taxes.

Let's take the case above again, but this time a bit slower. Let's consider just one year. In that year the property sustained a loss of $7,000 (primarily from depreciation). That $7,000 was then deducted from the investor's ordinary income. That meant that the investor avoided paying ordinary income taxes (read "high tax rate") on $7,000.

Now the very next year, that property sold, and it showed a $7,000 capital gain attributable to depreciation. The investor now had to pay tax on this amount. However, because it was a "capital gain" as opposed to "ordinary income," the tax rate was lower. Thus the great tax shelter benefit of real estate was that it converted ordinary income to capital gain and reduced the tax rate.

TIP

We're not talking here about the up-to-$500,000 exclusion on the sale of a personal residence by a married couple filing jointly. *That applies only to your main home.* Here, we're talking about investment property.

How the Capital Gain Is Calculated Now

Accounting for taxes on capital gain has changed in two ways. The first is that the Tax Reform Act of 1986 disqualified high-income investors from taking a deduction off their ordinary income for their real estate losses. Then the Taxpayer Relief Act of 1997 reduced the capital gains rate (and added a few more wrinkles, as we'll see shortly).

To begin, however, let's consider the rules with regard to taking a loss from real estate as a deduction against your ordinary income.

Active Income. The tax rule now discriminates between the types of income that we receive. Income we receive as wages or as compensation for services is called *active income.* It includes such income as commissions, consulting fees, and salaries. It's important for those involved in real estate to note that profits and losses from businesses in which you "materially participate" (not included are limited partnerships) are included. *However, activities from real estate are specifically excluded.*

Passive Income. This is a bit trickier to define, but in general it means the profit or loss that we receive from a business activity in which we do not materially participate. This includes not only limited partnerships but also income from any real estate that is rented out. It's important to remember that real estate investment income is specifically defined as *passive.*

Portfolio Income. This is income from dividends, interest, royalties, and anything similar. We need not worry much about this here except to note that it does not include real estate income.

Under the old rule, income was income and loss was loss. You could thus deduct any loss on real estate from your other income. Under the current rule your personal income is considered "active" while your real estate loss is considered "passive." Since you can't deduct a passive loss from active income, you can't, in general, write off any real estate losses whether from real expenses or from depreciation.

The Little Guy

We've already said that this tax code revision was aimed primarily at the wealthy to eliminate a big tax shelter. But there is an advantage to be retained here for the small investor.

There is an important exception to the above rule. This exception provides up to a $25,000 allowance for write-offs for those with lower ordinary income. In other words, you can write off up to $25,000 in losses from real estate against your active income, provided that you meet an income ceiling (plus certain other qualifications).

Your Gross Adjusted Income. This figure must not exceed $150,000. If your income is below $100,000, then you qualify for the entire $25,000 exception. If it is between $100,000 and $150,000, you lose 50 cents of the allowance for every dollar your income exceeds $100,000. The following table will help explain this.

Since most small investors have incomes under $150,000, the allowance applies to them. They can deduct their losses on real estate up to the $25,000 limitation.

Phasing Out the $25,000 Allowance as Income Increases

INCOME	ALLOWANCE	INCOME	ALLOWANCE	INCOME	ALLOWANCE
$100,000	$25,000	$117,000	$16,500	$134,000	$8,000
101,000	24,500	118,000	16,000	135,000	7,500
102,000	24,000	119,000	15,500	136,000	7,000
103,000	23,500	120,000	15,000	137,000	6,500
104,000	23,000	121,000	14,500	138,000	6,000
105,000	22,500	122,000	14,000	139,000	5,500
106,000	22,000	123,000	13,500	140,000	5,000
107,000	21,500	124,000	13,000	141,000	4,500
108,000	21,000	125,000	12,500	142,000	4,000
109,000	20,500	126,000	12,000	143,000	3,500
110,000	20,000	127,000	11,500	144,000	3,000
111,000	19,500	128,000	11,000	145,000	2,500
112,000	19,000	129,000	10,500	146,000	2,000
113,000	18,500	130,000	10,000	147,000	1,500
114,000	18,000	131,000	9,500	148,000	1,000
115,000	17,500	132,000	9,000	149,000	500
116,000	17,000	133,000	8,500	150,000	0

The Other Qualification. Earlier we said there is another qualification. It is that you must actively participate in the business of renting the property.

This can be tricky—after all, what does *actively participate* really mean?

Obviously if you own the property and are the only person directly involved in handling the rental—you advertise it, rent it, handle maintenance and clean-up, collect the rent, and so on— then you materially participate.

However, there are gray zones. Generally if you don't personally determine the rental terms, approve new tenants, sign for repairs, or approve capital improvements and the like, then you may not qualify.

The question always comes up, "What if I hire a management firm to handle the property for me?"

In general, a management firm is probably okay to use as long as you continue to materially participate (determine rental terms, approve new tenants, sign for repairs or capital improvements, and the like). If you qualify under the income restrictions and are going to use a management firm, be sure that you have your attorney check over the agreement you sign with the firm to see that it does not characterize you as not materially participating and thus prevent you from deducting any loss.

Other Kinks in the Rules. On the surface, the allowance and the qualifications may seem straightforward. But they can be tricky. For example, here are some other considerations:

1. The income used to determine whether you qualify is your *gross adjusted income*. This means your income after you have taken some deductions such as some retirement plan contributions (not IRAs), alimony, or moving expenses.
2. The allowance does not apply to farms. If you materially participate in the running of a farm, other rules apply— see your accountant or tax attorney.
3. Those who don't qualify for taking the deduction against their active income cannot likewise take the deduction against their portfolio income. (Remember, portfolio income comes from interest, dividends, royalties, and similar sources.)

So When I Sell, I Could Owe Some Capital Gains Taxes?

Yes, assuming you don't sell for a loss. However, as noted, the federal capital gains tax rate has been reduced. At the present time it's a maximum of 15 percent. Hence, even if you do have to pay, it won't be a confiscatory amount (State capital gains taxes are paid seperately.)

TRAP

You owe tax on a capital gain regardless of whether the property is an investment or a personal residence. However, if you sell at a capital loss, while you can take that loss on investment property, you can't take a deduction against that loss if it's on a personal residence! It's a quirk in the tax rules.

Is There Any Legal Way to Avoid Owing Taxes on My Profits?

That, of course, is the national pastime that most Americans play—how to legally avoid paying high taxes. And in the case of investment real estate, there are a few loopholes that can benefit the investor.

Using the Property as a Personal Residence

The first method that might be used is to convert the property from an investment to a personal residence. You can remove the tenants and move in yourself, declaring the property your principal residence. After a period of time, you may then be able to sell the home and reap the benefits of the principal residence capital gains exclusion of up to $500,000 for married couples filing jointly. (See Chapter 19 for more information on the exclusion.)

TIP

Keep in mind that in real estate you owe taxes on your profit (capital gain) *only when you sell*. No matter how high the value of your property goes, you don't pay tax on the gain as long as you continue to own it. (You would, of course, owe income taxes if you showed excess income over expenses on an annual basis, and you would owe annual property taxes.)

There are certain problems with the above scenario, however. The first is, how long must you reside in the property to make it your personal residence? I don't know of any hard-and-fast rule.

Some accountants say two years, others longer. Check with your professional tax advisor.

The second has to do with all that depreciation taken while you owned the property. Under the current rule, it is recaptured at a special rate. Thus, even though you may avoid paying taxes on most of your capital gain by using the personal property exclusion (noted earlier), you might still owe some taxes on the recaptured depreciation losses that you earlier took.

TRAP

Another wrinkle is the rule that if you previously used a Section 1031 tax-deferred exchange on a property that you then convert to a rental, you must own and reside it in it for the full five years before you get to claim the exclusion.

Trading to Legally Defer Paying Taxes on the Capital Gain

You can trade your investment property for another and defer the capital gain from the old property to the new. This is technically called a Section 1031(a)(3) tax-deferred exchange.

A great many investors see this as a means of multiplying their profits without paying taxes along the way. They hopscotch from property to property increasing the value of their real estate holdings unencumbered by paying taxes for each transaction.

TIP

It's sort of like getting compound interest on your equity. Normally, in a strict sale and then purchase of another property, you would pay taxes on your capital gain. That would leave you less equity to invest in the next property. However, by deferring that tax bill into the future, you have all your equity to put into the next property, meaning you can buy a bigger and better investment property!

The rules for a tax-free exchange are complex and are beyond the scope of this book. They were codified several decades ago by tax cases, the most famous of which is called the *Starker rule*. Under a Starker delayed exchange, you just go ahead and sell your investment property as you would otherwise to any buyer. However, you have 45 days after the sale to designate a new property(ies) into which you will invest your money. And then you have 180 days to close the deal on that new property(ies) (the timelines run concurrently). A recent amendment allows you time before the sale to designate a new property. Also, there are specific restrictions when it comes to identifying properties. (You can trade one or more properties for one or more other properties.)

Note: While it's called a "trade" or an "exchange," you do not need to sell your property to the seller of the property you buy. Rather you can sell your property to anyone . . . and buy another property from anyone. To get the full deferral, however, the new property(ies) must be of equal or greater value than the old property(ies).

Note that there are other strict conditions of the exchange that must be met. One is that to defer all you'll gain, you may not take cash out ("boot") as part of the sale. If you want cash out, you usually refinance the new property after the exchange.

Also only like-kind properties can be exchanged. *Like kind* for our purposes usually means property held for business or investment purposes. Thus you not only would be able to exchange a rental house for another rental house but also for an apartment house, an office building, or even bare land. On the other hand, exchanging an apartment building for a principal residence would not be allowed by the IRS.

Combining an Exchange with a Personal Property Exclusion

One of the problems with converting an investment property into a personal property to take advantage of the residence exclusion is that you may not want to reside in a property you own as an investment. If that's the case, then the answer could be to do a tax-deferred exchange of the investment property into one in which you would like to live. Then convert the desirable home from investment to principal residence. Just remember that now you must reside in the property for five years, not just two out of five years, to get the exclusion.

Keep in mind, however, the like-kind rule noted above. A personal residence is not the same as an investment house. Therefore, in order to not invalidate the tax-deferred status of the exchange, you might have to rent out the new property for a time before moving in yourself. How long before converting to a principal residence? Some tax advisors have suggested six months, others as long as two years. Again, check with your own professional tax advisor.

What Type of Records Do I Need to Keep?

From our discussion here, one other thing should be apparent: You need to keep good records. It's very important that you keep every receipt and note every expense and piece of income in a ledger.

You may have to prove to the IRS that expenses that you had on your investment property were real. For example, three years earlier you had a vacancy and you spent $115 on advertising to get a new tenant.

Prove it, says the IRS. So you reach into your bag of receipts and pull out an invoice from the local paper for $115 for advertising. Attached to it is a copy of the ad itself and your check in payment. It's hard to dispute that.

Also, keep all records if you make improvements to the property. Remember, improvements *raise* the tax basis, which will later reduce the amount of capital gain and ultimately capital gains taxes you will need to pay. (The higher the tax basis, the lower the capital gain.)

If you make a capital improvement, such as put on a new roof or add a patio, keep all of the receipts. At the end of the year your accountant will be able to use them to adjust your tax basis upward.

TIP

Just because you spend money improving your rental, it doesn't mean that you've made a capital improvement for tax purposes. Replacing a water heater, for example, usually is not a capital improvement; it's a repair. Adding a tile roof where there was previously a less expensive tar roof would be a capital improvement (at least the difference in price between the tar roof and the tile).

What If I Refinance?

As strange as it may seem, refinancing your property without a sale has no immediate tax consequences. You don't report new mortgages to the IRS. You will, however, have less equity to rely on later when you do sell and must pay capital gains taxes.

If I've conveyed nothing else to you in this chapter, I hope that I have given the impression that buying and selling real estate goes hand in hand with tax considerations. If you're a wise investor, you'll consult with your tax professional each time *before* you make a new move.

Index

About the Author

ROBERT IRWIN is one of America's foremost experts in every area of real estate. He is the author of McGraw-Hill's bestselling Tips and Traps series, as well as *The Home Buyer's Checklist, How to Get Started in Real Estate Investing,* and *How to Buy a Home When You Can't Afford It.* His books have sold more than one million copies. Visit his Web site at www.robertirwin.com.